JIMI
HENDRIX

THE ILLUSTRATED

JIMI HENDRIX

GEOFFREY GIULIANO
BRENDA GIULIANO
and
DEBORAH LYNN BLACK

SUNBURST BOOKS

DEDICATION

This work is dedicated to Caesar Glebbeek for his tireless devotion in helping to preserve the music and memory of Jimi Hendrix. For over twenty-five years he has assisted fans worldwide with great good humour and the attention to detail found only in true professionals. For this particular book he acted as photo researcher, secondary editor and overall project co-ordinator.

Caesar Glebbeek is co-author of the definitive biography, *Jimi Hendrix: Electric Gypsy* and editor of *UniVibes, International Jimi Hendrix Magazine*.

And to Sesa, a real electric lady.

GG and BG

Text copyright © Indigo Editions Ltd. 1994
Design copyright © Sunburst Books 1994

This edition published 1994 by Sunburst Books,
Deacon House, 65 Old Church Street, London SW3 5BS.

ISBN 1 85778 035 3

Printed and bound in China

CONTENTS

CHAPTER ONE

BOLD AS LOVE: EARLY LIFE

"My earliest memory was of being in the hospital. The nurse changed my diapers and afterwards held me up to the window. I could see the sky and there were fireworks. It must have been the Fourth of July."
Jimi Hendrix

Jimi's paternal grandmother, Nora Rose Hendrix.

FIREWORKS WERE DESTINED to surround him his entire life. Little James Allen Hendrix was born into a world at war at 10.15 am on 27th November, 1942 at Seattle's King County Hospital. For his mother, the former Lucille Jeter, barely eighteen and in delicate health, it was hardly a time for celebration. She had no money, no home and her new husband was off to war. Baby Jimmy** was facing a future of instability that would mark his childhood and affect much of his adult life.

Meanwhile, James Allen Hendrix, a private in the US Army based in Alabama, was in the stockade when the news of the arrival of his first born son reached him. "Under army regulations I was entitled to furlough to see my child," explains Al. "But my commanding officer said I lived too far away. I was put in the stockade when I hadn't done anything wrong. General principles, they said."

In fact, it was three years before Al was finally discharged and made his way to California to pick up his son who had been in the care of a friend of Lucille's mother, a kindly woman named Mrs. Champ. From the letters Al had received from Jimi's guardian, it appeared to Al that Jimi's life was an unsavory one of being shunted around amongst friends and relatives, frequently living in shoddy hotels and rooming-houses. Lucille, wild, young and clearly not ready for motherhood, began drinking heavily and had taken to running around with a bad crowd that included a notorious abuser of women, who once beat Lucille so badly that she ended up in hospital for an extended period.

*[** Author's note: From his youngest days Hendrix was called by the standard diminutive of James, although in those days the spelling would almost certainly have been the conventional "Jimmy." In this book however I have used the spelling adopted by Jimi throughout his professional career.]*

Nora Hendrix's 100th birthday celebration on 19th November, 1983.
Left to right: Pearl Brown (Jimi's aunt), Nora Hendrix, Jimi's father.

As for Jimi, the frequent moves from one cold, damp boarding house to another inevitably took their toll. He later recalled, "I had pneumonia when I was young and I used to scream and cry every time they put the needle in me."

When he saw his three-year-old boy for the first time, Al remembers being slightly distressed, "Mrs. Champ was very reluctant to give him up," he says. "She sure did love him. He'd become part of her family. Even though they told him about me, showed him my picture, when I got there it was a very strange feeling, to see your own kid and he's talking and walking and doesn't know you."

Back in Seattle Al was reunited with Lucille. Together the family settled down and for the first time Jimi enjoyed the love and affection of a real family. In November, 1946, Al Hendrix changed his son's name to James Marshall Hendrix, Marshall in memory of Al's brother, Leon Marshall, who had died in 1932.

Around this time music entered his young life. Show biz, after all was in his blood. His paternal grandmother, Nora Hendrix, of Cherokee descent, had traveled throughout British Columbia as a chorus girl with a vaudeville troupe. Al himself was a veteran of the local Vancouver circuit, tap dancing with the touring shows that hit town and improvising to the dance crazes of the day in his oversized zoot suit. In fact, both Al and Lucille were fairly serious dancers. The couple first met at a dance where Fats Waller was playing.

Lucille, the local Seattle jitterbug champion standing a diminutive five feet, was a perfect match for Al who was only two inches taller. Together the couple became a popular entry at the many dance contests throughout central Seattle. Jimi remembers watching his parents practising their routines in the living room to the swinging sounds of Duke Ellington, Count Basie, and the energetic R&B stomp of Louis Jordan.

Jimi aged three, 1945.

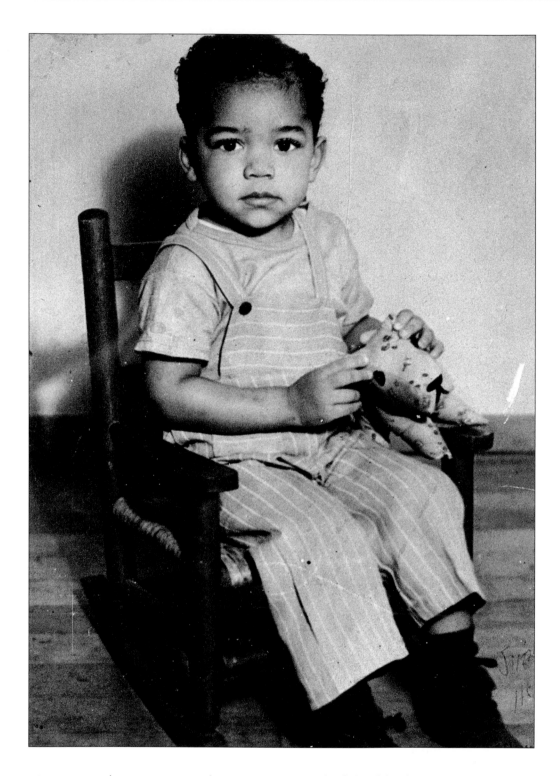

   Jimi was also witness to the rousing sound of the black Pentecostal Church. As a child he often sang hymns at the Church of God and Christ, accompanied by jug-band sounds, harmonica, guitar and tambourine. "The music just seemed to engulf me and carry me away," Hendrix once said. "It went through me from my head to my feet."
   By the time Jimi started kindergarten, the Hendrixs moved into the Ranier Vista Housing Project. Al had gone back to school under the GI Bill to train as an electrician and worked nights as a janitor while Lucille looked after Jimi and his baby brother Leon, who was born in January, 1948.

Shortly thereafter, however, things began to deteriorate. Money was perpetually tight, and a restless Lucille, ever in search of a good time, would often disappear for days on end. Over the next three years Jimi and Leon were witness to numerous explosive arguments which often led to volatile separations and tearful reunions.

Leon recalls one particularly unhappy occasion when Al found their mother with another man. "She got in our car and we left. She was really drunk. Dad was shouting at her, 'Act right! Grow up! Behave y'self!' Mom got mad and reached over with her foot, hit the gas and then the brake. The car jumped forward then stopped short and me and Jimi flew into the front seat. Mom was crying and telling us she was sorry. She hugged us and loved us up. That was the most love I ever got from her. Probably Jimi too."

In a rare reference to those tumultuous days, Hendrix once commented, "My mother and father used to fight a lot and I always had to be ready to go tippy-toeing off to Canada. My dad was level-headed and reli-

Above: Leon and Jimi in Seattle, 1950.

Right: Jimi at the age of three in Seattle, mid 1946.

gious, but my mother used to like having a good time and dressing up. She used to drink a lot and didn't take care of herself. But she was a groovy mother."

The tempestuous, ill-fated marriage inevitably ended in divorce in December, 1951, with Al gaining custody of his two boys along with a third son, Joseph, about whom little is known. Joseph was born in 1949 and was subsequently fostered out. Jimi and Leon were often left alone to fend for themselves while their father performed a series of menial jobs and moved the family from one dreary rooming-house to another, trying his best to keep the Welfare Department at bay. Often the brothers were shunted among relatives and friends, interspersed with occasional heartbreaking visits to their mother.

Al remembers, "Jimi would say to me, 'Why does Mamma always tell me she's gonna do this and that when she knows she's not gonna be able to do it?....' When we broke up she'd come by to see the kids

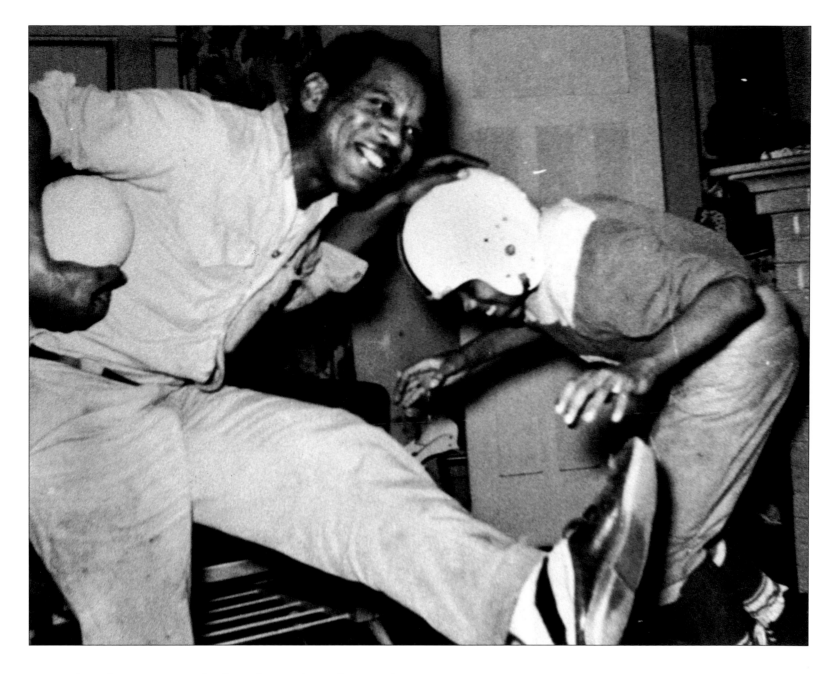

around twelve or one o'clock in the night. I'd say, 'This ain't no time to be coming to see the kids, they're in bed now.' She said, 'Oh yeah, yeah.'"

Al and Jimi having some fun on Hallowe'en in Seattle, 29th November, 1956.

Eventually Al simply couldn't cope with the two children and placed Leon in a foster home. During the next five years he was to be in seven foster homes. However, this move proved to be a blow to Jimi, whose brother was the only constant security he'd known. Always a quiet, sensitive youngster he now became painfully withdrawn and developed a fairly bad stutter. Retreating into a world of fantasy, he would often put on a makeshift cape and helmet and race through the neighborhood, a sci-fi hero from the mythical planet Mongo, out to save the earth from evil Ming the Merciless. At school, though, his escape was poetry and art.

"I used to write poetry a lot and then I was really happy," he says. "My poems were mostly about flowers, nature and people wearing robes. I

"We won all the games!" Jimi and his coach in November, 1956.

wanted to be an actor or a painter. The teacher used to say, 'Paint three scenes' and I'd do abstract stuff like the Martian sunset or a summer afternoon on Venus." Already Jimi was developing his own inner world which would later heavily influence his songwriting.

By the age of twelve Jimi was already showing signs of having a significant talent for music. As a young child he picked up the spoons from his father and by the age of eight became obsessed with strumming on the household broom, singing Elvis Presley songs like *Heartbreak Hotel* and *Love Me Tender*.

Mr. Hendrix remembers Jimi's first "guitar" - "He'd be sweeping the floor and he'd sit at the end of the bed and make believe it was a guitar. I'd see all this straw on the floor and I said, 'I thought you were supposed to have swept the floor!' So he had to sweep up again."

"Jimi would walk down the street with that broom singing the notes and pretending to play," remembers Leon. "He'd even take it to school. Everyone thought he was crazy." In fact, a social worker, convinced that the lack of a guitar was damaging to the young student, tried to get him a proper instrument paid for out of a special fund for needy children.

The school authorities, however, remained unconvinced.

"I tried to teach him some dance steps but he wasn't much of a dancer," notes Al. "His hands were good, though, so once when I was doing some yardwork, cleaning garages and such as that, I found an old ukelele and took it home. I had to get some strings for it though. This was around 1955. He'd play that ukelele sometimes right-handed, sometimes left-handed. I guess he figured he'd do better left-handed and that's what he did."

Just as Jimi was beginning to really express himself he suffered another blow. His mother, Lucille, newly married to a longshoreman in December, 1957, was in and out of hospital suffering from cirrhosis of the liver. Jimi often snuck off to see her, proudly showing her the artwork he'd done in school.

"He did a lot of drawing," remembers Al. "He drew one of me while I was sleeping. He had a good imagination. He always thought about becoming a commercial artist, because it was something he could do with his hands."

Early in 1958 Lucille was back in the hospital, seriously ill. This time Jimi's Aunt Pat, Al's sister, down from Vancouver, took her nephew to see his mother. Jimi was very quiet and simply stared. It was the last time he ever saw his mother. On 2nd February, 1958, Lucille died of a ruptured spleen brought on by a failing liver. Jimi did not attend the funeral, ostensibly because there was no one to take him. It appears, however, that Al, still deeply embittered over his former wife, stubbornly refused to allow Jimi to go.

In later years Hendrix recalled a vivid dream: "My mother was being carried away on this camel. It was a big caravan and she's going under these trees and you could see the shade, you know the leaf patterns across her face. She's saying 'Well, I won't be seeing you too much anymore you know. I'll see you.' And I said, 'Yeah, but where are you going?' It was about two years after that she died. I will always remember that. There are some dreams you never forget."

At the tender age of fifteen the emotionally fragile young Jimi Hendrix had lost his mother. But in the wake of that great sorrow a rare talent was about to awaken. In the year of his mother's death Jimi Hendrix got his first guitar.

"Jimi was a dreamer. I guess that's what made him so great."
Al Hendrix

CHAPTER TWO

BEYOND THE WILL OF GOD: MUSICAL VISIONS

"I hear music in my head all the time. Sometimes it makes my brain throb and the room starts to turn. I feel I'm going mad. With this music we will paint pictures of earth and space so that the listener can be taken somewhere."
Jimi Hendrix

Jimi during his training period at Fort Ord, California, 20th June, 1961.

AS A YOUNG CHILD Jimi would often tag along with his father to all-night card games with the boys. As luck would have it, one of Al's poker buddies had an acoustic guitar which almost immediately became an obsession with Jimi. Jimi would sneak the guitar out to the porch and be lost in another world until it was time to leave.

"I didn't know I would have to put the strings around the other way because I was left-handed. I can remember thinking to myself, 'There's something wrong here.' I finally changed the strings around, but I didn't know a thing about tuning. So I went down to the store and ran my fingers across the strings on a guitar they had there. After that I was able to tune my own."

Meanwhile, Jimi was devouring virtually every blues record he could lay his hands on: Howlin' Wolf, Muddy Waters, B.B. King and the legendary Robert Johnson. Hendrix remembers, "The first guitarist I was really aware of was Muddy Waters. I heard one of his old records when I was a little boy and it scared me to death."

Slowly, painstakingly, he would pick away at the guitar trying to imitate the sounds he heard. "He used to practise a lot," says Al. "I'd come home from work and he'd be there, "plunk, plunk, plunk." He taught himself. It was just in him. The guitar became another part of his anatomy."

Not long afterwards, Al bought Jimi a white Supro Ozark electric. At the same time, Mr. Hendrix picked up a saxophone and father and son would often play wild duets. These happy occasions formed a bond between them. As a strict disciplinarian, Al often found it difficult to express his emotions to Jimi and music provided them with some common ground.

"The way I felt about tap dancing is the way Jimi felt about guitar playing," admits Al proudly. "I could almost see his vision of himself playing for a group. I mean, finally that's what he did too."

Jimi joined his first band in 1959, The Velvetones. Jimi didn't stay with

them for very long, as, a few months later, he joined The Rocking Kings. Rather than play lead, Hendrix played bass on a six-string guitar. The group's first gig was in Kent, just outside Seattle at the National Guard Armory. "We earned thirty-five cents apiece," Hendrix recalled. "We used to play stuff by The Coasters. In those days I just liked rock'n'roll I guess."

Under the management of local guitarist, James Thomas, the band played dances and parties all over town and was even placed second in the 1960 All State Band of the Year competition. The group's biggest break, however, was when they became resident at Birdland, playing the Wednesday teenage dance nights. Named after the famous New York jazz club, Birdland was located in the black area of Seattle. It was here that Jimi's beloved guitar was stolen, prompting poor Al Hendrix to purchase his son a white Danelectro which he subsequently painted red.

The highlight of Jimi's tenure with The Rocking Kings came at an outdoor picnic at Cottage Lake, when the band played to a widely appreciative crowd of over 2,000. The gig was noted for Jimi's first public guitar gymnastics, freely playing behind his head and between his legs. He'd picked up the showmanship from Big Jay McNeely, a wild tenor sax player who played his instrument while lying on his back.

Left to right
Lester Exeano - Drums
James Hendrix - Guitar
Web Lofton - Sax
Walter Harris - Sax
Robert Green - Piano

TAKEN. Washington Hall
February 20, 1960

Top: Hendrix pictured playing his very first electric guitar, a cheap Supro Ozark, in the early Seattle band, The Rocking Kings.

Above: Jimi's own caption (calling himself James at that time), written on the back of the photo.

Above: Leon Morris Hendrix, Jimi's brother, in 1982.

Right: Jimi posing with Diane and Robert 'Bobby' Hendrix, Pearl's children, in Vancouver around 1960.

His rising local fame (and notoriety) brought a perk that was a Hendrix legend in the making. Willing young women literally flocked to his door. His father remembers keeping them at bay. "These girls would come by to go to church or something with him. I'd say, 'Oh, some little girl wants you...' He'd say, 'Oh, don't tell her I'm here.' 'Jeez, Jimi, she looks awful good to me.'"

Jimi had a steady girl, Betty Jean Morgan, whose name he had inscribed on his beloved guitar. Reportedly the relationship even progressed to the point of Hendrix giving her an engagement ring before the couple eventually parted.

By 1960 Hendrix was playing in a number of local bands including The Tom Cats. In addition, he would often hang around local clubs hoping for a chance to sit in. It scarcely mattered that the guitars were all right-handed. According to Leon, "It didn't really matter to Jimi. He'd turn the sucker upside down and play it better than the guy who owned it."

Unfortunately, Jimi's accomplishments in the classroom didn't match his prowess on the guitar. Apart from sports and art classes Jimi was a poor, generally disinterested student at Garfield High. Frequent absen-

Jimi clowning on stage at the Pink Poodle Club, Clarksville, Tennessee, November 1961. Billy Cox is on the right.

teeism and an all consuming interest in music finally led to Jimi's dropping out of Garfield in October of his senior year. The official reason for his departure was, "Work referral and age," but Hendrix later told the real story. "I had a girlfriend in art class and we used to hold hands all the time. The art teacher didn't dig that at all. She was very prejudiced. She said, 'Mr. Hendrix, I'll see you in the cloakroom in three seconds, please.' Back in the cloakroom she said, 'What do you mean talking to that white woman like that?' I said, 'Are you jealous?' She started crying and I got thrown out."

Life in the real world, Hendrix quickly discovered, didn't live up to his fantasies. Jimi tried to get a job as a bag boy at a local grocery, but according to Al, "That was before the civil rights thing and it was hard for blacks to get into certain jobs." Now a fairly successful landscaper, Mr. Hendrix took his son on as an assistant, but Jimi wasn't really cut out for manual labor and didn't like taking orders from his father.

"I had to carry stones and cement all day while he pocketed the money," recalls Hendrix. "I ran away after a blazing row with my dad. He hit me in the face and I ran away."

Unemployed and restless, with time on his hands, Jimi wandered into

Now here's a picture that was hard to take - I took this one comeing down and almost broke my friend's camera by landing - this was one of my bad landing's - he was pretty close to the ground when this was taken. Notice the snow -

Taken Feb 67, '6

March 5, 1962 - Jimmy

A jump school picture with a caption by Jimi himself!

Opposite: The King Kasuals, one of Jimi's early bands prior to his departure from the US Army a few months later, at the Jolly Roger club, Nashville, Tennessee, in spring 1962. Center: Billy Cox, right: Leonard Moses.

several unsavory situations. One night he and a few pals broke into Wilner's Clothing Store to cop a few sweaters, shirts and slacks. Explained Hendrix, "I was always gone on wearing hip clothes and the only way to get them was through the back window of the clothing store." Once the culprits were discovered, however, the owner declined to press charges after Al Hendrix offered him free gardening for a year.

Although Jimi had his fair share of street fights and petty scrapes with the law, James Oliver, a schoolmate at Garfield, reveals that Jimi was never really an instigator. "Jimi wouldn't really get involved that much. He didn't rip and run like we did. He wasn't an aggressive roughhouse like us. He was a shy type of guy. He only went along because it was easy."

On 2nd May, 1961, Jimi was arrested for joyriding in a stolen car and taken into custody by Seattle police. Just four days later he was arrested again and charged with "taking a motor vehicle without the owner's permission." The eighteen-year-old was subsequently jailed for seven days at the Rainier Vista 4-H Youth Center.

Jimi stood silently before the judge who sternly warned, "Son, I don't want to send you back to jail, but I don't want to see you here again.

Have you ever given any thought to enlisting in the army?"

Hendrix apparently took this advice to heart. He had no money, no job prospects, plus things weren't going at all well at home with his father. "Because I didn't have a cent in my pocket I walked into the first recruiting office I saw and went into the army." On 31st May, 1961, bidding a reluctant farewell to Betty Jean, he was bussed off to Fort Ord, California for eight weeks basic training.

Life in the service proved a heady experience for the new recruit when he was first assigned to the 101st Airborne Division at Fort Campbell, Kentucky. The glamour of paratrooping clearly captured his imagination and he spoke excitedly of his first jump: "It was really outta sight. You're there at the door and there's this rush and you're out like that and it's just "ooooooh." It's the most alone feeling in the world and every time you jump you're scared that maybe this time it won't open. Then you feel that tug on your collar and there's that big beautiful white mushroom above you and the air's going "sssshhhh" past our ears."

In January 1962 Jimi had his treasured Danelectro guitar shipped to him and he promptly took up the practice of sleeping with the instrument, following the example of Mississippi John Hurt. This, along with his aloof behavior, occasionally made him a target of derisive remarks and pranks, such as hiding his guitar. Once he was even attacked by fellow soldiers, only to be rescued by an old boxing friend from Seattle.

His service experience, however, was most remembered for his meeting with bass player, Billy Cox. Private Cox, sheltered just outside Service Club Number one, remembers hearing guitar sounds coming from inside he later described as, "Somewhere between Beethoven and John Lee Hooker" and went to investigate. "Jimi was limited to about five keys and was still getting his shit together," noted Cox, "but I said, 'Wow, the cat's all right!' So I stepped in and introduced myself. I told him I played bass and we started jamming right off."

Hendrix and Cox soon became the nucleus of two top service groups; one a five-piece band called The King Kasuals, and the second, a trio that played the service clubs and army bases throughout North and South Carolina. It was Jimi's weekend passes to Nashville, however, that opened up a whole new musical experience. By night Billy and Jimi cruised the city's watering holes and by day toured local recording studios, thoroughly captivated by the burgeoning music scene. Jimi vowed he would cut a record when he left the service.

Having earned his coveted Screaming Eagle paratrooper patch, PFC James Marshall Hendrix finally found a way out of the service. "One day I got my ankle caught in the sky hook just as I was going to jump and I broke it. I told them I hurt my back too. Every time they examined me I groaned, so they finally believed me and I got out."

In July of 1962, discharge papers in hand, Jimi headed for nearby Clarksville, where, two months later, Billy Cox joined him, and together they reformed The King Kasuals to work the Nashville club circuit. To make ends meet they also backed obscure artists with wild names like Nappy Brown, School Boy, and Ironing Board Sam. Hendrix also managed to join a tour with The Marvellettes and Curtis Mayfield. Jimi learned much of the art of resonance and pulse from Mayfield, whose

Jimi playing a Fender Duo-Sonic during a club date with Curtis Knight And The Squires, New York, late 1965.
Left to right: Jimi, Ed Dantes, Curtis Knight.

tasteful playing influenced the more melodic aspects of Hendrix own unique style.

The next two years found a struggling Hendrix playing the all black "chitlin circuit," finding himself on the bill with the likes of Sam Cooke, Jackie Wilson and Little Richard. Hendrix would often improvise guitar licks to relieve the boredom, only to be glared back into line for diverting attention away from the star.

As the winter of 1963 set in, Jimi returned to Nashville. He was playing the local Baron club one evening, when an out of town promoter walked in and convinced the young guitarist he could become a star in New York. Reasoning he had gone about as far on the Nashville circuit as he could, Jimi saw the opportunity to move on.

Far from his vision of the bright lights of Broadway, Hendrix found himself in Harlem just one among hundreds of hopeful musicians trying to catch a break in the big city. Jimi's striking looks drew the attention of streetwise Faye Pridgeon. A famous groupie who'd had affairs with many of the top musicians that played the Apollo Theater, Faye took Jimi home to her mother's Central Park apartment.

"Jimi always loved fooling about with his guitar in bed and always slept with it. I used to think of my competition not as a woman, but as a guitar! Many times he fell asleep with it on his chest. Any time I tried to remove it he woke up and said, 'No, no, leave my guitar alone!' "

Faye recalled how one night at a Harlem club someone was pestering her for a dance when a jealous Hendrix leapt off the stage and whacked the guy on the head with his guitar. Of his violent streak he once admitted, "No matter how sweet and lovely you are, there are black and ugly things deep down somewhere."

Faye's connections got Jimi a coveted spot on Amateur Night at the Apollo where he took home the first place prize of $25.00. By Christmas of 1963 at the age of twenty-one he got his first chance to record, when he was hired for sessions with saxophone player, Lonnie Youngblood, in Philadelphia. These early Hendrix recordings, like *Wipe The Sweat* and *Under The Table*, demonstrate his distinctive vibration and astonishingly mature blues guitar style.

In March, 1964, Jimi was playing in the house band of Harlem's Palm Cafe, when in walked Tony Rice, a friend of the renowned Isley Brothers. The band was in need of a new guitarist and Rice told Ronnie Isley to look no further; he'd found their man. One audition was all The Isleys needed and Jimi was in.

The first order of business was to record a single on The Isleys' new T-Neck label. The song, *Testify*, was full of Hendrix's hard-driving rhythm chords and fluid blues-inspired breaks. Another single, *The Last Girl* b/w *Looking For A Love*, also featured Jimi's distinctive guitar.

Going out on tour with The Isleys, Ronnie relates an early episode. "We heard what sounded like a riot going on and figured one of the local acts must have had a big hit. So we all peeked out from the dressing room and there was Jimi, down on his knees biting his guitar and the crowd were just going crazy."

"They used to let me do my thing," said Hendrix, "because it made them more bucks."

Although The Isleys allowed Jimi to shun the band uniform for Zebra sunglasses, frilly shirts and skin tight trousers, along with a certain amount of on stage freewheeling, he was still not his own boss. Ditching the band in Nashville, he hooked up once again with Little Richard and played on the single, I Don't Know What You've Got But It's Got Me, which unfortunately hardly dented the charts. On tour it quickly became apparent that the megalomaniac Richard wasn't going to stand for his young guitarist's attention grabbing antics.

Hendrix remarks, "He told me, 'I am Little Richard and I am the King of Rock'n'Rhythm and I'm the one who's going to look pretty on stage! Take off that frilly shirt or else you will suffer the consequences of a fine.' He had yet another meeting over my hairstyle. I said I wasn't going to cut my hair for nobody." Jimi soon left Little Richard.

By autumn 1965 Hendrix hooked up with Curtis Knight and The Squires, a Top Forty R&B band which was reasonably well known on the dance club circuit. Knight promptly introduced his new guitarist to record producer Ed Chalpin, who immediately signed the naive, over-eager young artist to an exclusive three-year contract with his PPX Enterprises in exchange for one dollar and a one per cent royalty after studio expenses. It was a deal that would remain a yoke around Jimi's neck for the remainder of his brief life.

With The Squires, Hendrix was finally afforded the freedom to express his developing sound. The hallmark of Hendrix's tenure with The Squires was the live material recorded at George's Club 20 in Hackensack, New Jersey. The recordings feature Jimi's full range of the blues, from delicate poetic strokes to a maniacal frenzy, bordering on the psychedelic sound that was just around the corner. "I play the blues like they never heard!" he wrote in a postcard to Al in January, 1966.

Musicians were now taking notice of this maverick young guitar slinger. Early in 1966, King Curtis, the top sax session man in the business, whose wailing solo made the Coasters' *Yakety Sax* a monster hit, was searching for a second guitarist for his band, The Kingpins. As Hendrix was brought into the fold, Bernard Purdie, primo drummer for the group, remembers his first gig without the benefit of any rehearsal. "He knew everything, so he didn't have any problem. On a lot of songs that Jimi didn't know the bass player had to whisper the chords to him. But I never in my life saw anybody pick up songs as Jimi did that night."

With seasoned players like Curtis, Purdie, bassist Chuck Rainey and lead guitarist Cornell Dupree, some critics suggested that this may have been the best early band Hendrix ever played with. The pile-driving R&B with jazz overtones, demanding and challenging, was marked by Jimi's debut with his new Fender Stratocaster.

King Curtis, however, was also a strict taskmaster, whose rigid rules and regulations deemed shirt cuffs must be folded over jacket sleeves. For the free spirited Hendrix, such trivial restrictions were just too much. It was once again time to jump ship.

Something else was happening too. Disillusioned by the uneventful, formula gigs with The Kingpins and Squires, the role of sideman was one he had clearly outgrown. Jimi had revolutionary musical ideas which could no longer be suppressed. Leaving Harlem behind, he moved to Greenwich Village to form his own band. The world was on the verge of discovering one of the greatest rock guitarists of all time.

"When Jimi was last here in Seattle he said, 'I'm going to make you proud of me.' But I can't be more proud of him than I am now."
Al Hendrix

CHAPTER THREE

TURN THE TIDES: FINDING A VOICE

"I had these dreams that something was gonna happen, seeing the number 1966 in my sleep, so I was just passing time till then. I wanted my own scene, making my music, not playing the same old riffs."

Jimi Hendrix

CALLING HIMSELF JIMMY JAMES, after gospel great Junior Parker, Hendrix assembled a motley crew of white musicians from Greenwich Village for his first band, The Blue Flames. The dark basement of the hip Cafe Wha? on MacDougal Street at last provided the ideal format for Jimi to unleash his creative ideas. His repertoire ranged from urban blues, pop and progressive R&B to a freaky sound with strange, guttural feedback balanced against peaking riffs.

Mike Bloomfield of the Chicago based Paul Butterfield Blues Band was very impressed. "Jimi told me he knew he could do more on the guitar than anybody he ever heard. Hendrix was laying things on me that were more sounds than they were licks. H-bombs were going off, guided missiles were flying. As many times as I watched him play I couldn't figure out what he was doing. His thumb was so big, his hands so outsized nothing looked orthodox. Even when he played songs like Like a Rolling Stone, where I really knew the chords I could never connect what he was doing with his hands with what I was hearing."

Among the many well known patrons of Cafe Wha? was Linda Keith, a London fashion model and girlfriend of Rolling Stones guitarist Keith Richards. Watching Hendrix perform, her instincts told her that here was star material and she knew just the man to make it happen. Chas Chandler, bassist for The Animals was in New York on a farewell tour and was on the lookout for acts to manage, along with his partner Michael Jeffery. Linda excitedly took him down to the club where Jimi was playing a wild version of Billy Roberts' *Hey Joe*. Coincidentally it was the very song Chandler wanted to cover in England to launch his business career. After Jimi's set Chandler promptly sat the guitarist down and told him, "I believe you'll be a great sensation in England. If you

Opposite: Jimi's first trip to Germany. The Big Apple club in Munich, November 1966.

An early club gig at the Bag O' Nails pub, London, 25th November, 1966.

An advertisement for an early gig. Note the mispelling of Jimi's name.

agree I'll pay your fare to London, look after you and manage your affairs."

"Well, if you take me to England you've gotta take me to meet Eric Clapton," Jimi demanded, and this was apparently the clincher that sealed the deal.

Within days of their arrival in London, Chandler kept his promise and arranged for Jimi to not only meet Clapton, but to jam with him and the newly formed Cream at the Regent Street Polytechnic. Cream founder, Ginger Baker, wasn't particularly enthusiastic, but reluctantly agreed. "I could see Jimi was a really brilliant player, no denying it. But when he started in on his antics, dropping to his knees, playing the guitar with his teeth, I wasn't impressed. In Cream we were musicians. We didn't need this stuff."

Eric, on the other hand, remembers being blown away. "I think he played a Howlin' Wolf number, *Killing Floor*, but he did his whole routine, playing the guitar with his teeth, layin' on the floor, playin' behind

his head and doin' the splits, the whole thing. I turned to Chas and said is he that good? It was incredible."

Those first days in London were also significant for Jimi's meeting with stunning nineteen-year-old Kathy Etchingham, one of three women who would figure prominently in his life. Kathy recalls their first encounter in the Scotch of St. James club. "He leaned towards me, kissed my ear and said, 'I think you're beautiful.' He was terribly polite, I've never met anyone more well mannered in my life. We started going around all the time together and I moved into the hotel with him. We were very much wrapped up with one another." The couple would be together for the best part of two years, the longest relationship with a woman that Hendrix ever had.

Another woman who was to become a prominent figure in Hendrix's life was Devon Wilson, who claimed to have given Jimi his

Above: The Jimi Hendrix Experience live in London at the very beginning.

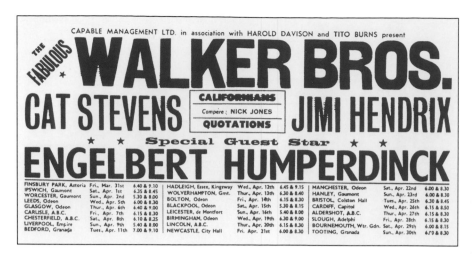

What a line-up!

first LSD. Wilson was an obsessive, self-destructive figure who manipulated Hendrix both in and out of the studio.. Although at one stage Devon considered herself as Jimi's bride-to-be Al Hendrix remembers things differently. "She used to tell me that her and Jimi were going to get married. Well, I knew different. These 'pick-up-kind-of-girls' he used to go with, Jimi don't want no girl like that."

Meanwhile, Chas Chandler's top priority was to put together a band for Jimi and get him into the studio. Noel Redding was first on board, a young guitarist who had toured with The Hollies and Manfred Mann. Currently going nowhere with his own band, The Loving Kind, the disillusioned Redding was about to give it all up to become a milkman when he decided to audition for Eric Burdon's new Animals. The spot was already taken, but instead, Chandler offered Redding the bass spot with Jimi and just like that, he was in.

Hendrix liked to joke that it was Redding's Afro hairstyle that got him the gig, but explained, "He played what I considered a steady bass and felt I could communicate with Noel." Possibly it also meant Jimi liked the idea of a novice bassist whom he could mold to his own style.

The choice of drummers came down to two accomplished blues musicians, Aynsley Dunbar of John Mayall's Bluesbreakers and John 'Mitch' Mitchell who had been part of the outlandish mod band, Riot Squad, whose stage act included painted faces and exotic props. In the end it was decided by the toss of a coin with Mitchell winning the toss. "Man, when I saw that small young dude sitting behind that big double kit of his," recalled Hendrix, "I didn't think he could even reach the cymbals. But when he started to play I knew I'd found the drummer I was looking for. He had a very original style with power which I knew would go very good with my own kind of playing."

"It was the first time I'd worked in a trio and been able to play really loud," Mitch says. "It felt good to have the amount of freedom to play whatever you wanted within a small framework of people. I was a little blasé about Noel's playing to a degree, but he took care of business. I think he always wanted to be a guitarist more than a bass player but he certainly held things down more than adequately."

The finishing touch was the novel spelling of Jimi's name and in early October, 1966, the Jimi Hendrix Experience was born. The excited guitarist phoned home and proclaimed, "It's me Dad. Guess what? I'm in England. I've met some people and they're going to make me a big star. We changed my name to Jimi."

With little time to rehearse, The Experience was booked into a four-gig tour with French singing sensation Johnny Hallyday. Debuting at the Novelty Cinema in Evreux, Jimi was reluctantly thrust into the spotlight, singing lead on several soul standards. One reviewer commented, "Johnny Hallyday's latest discovery was a singer/guitar player with bushy hair, a bad mixture of James Brown and Chuck Berry who pulled

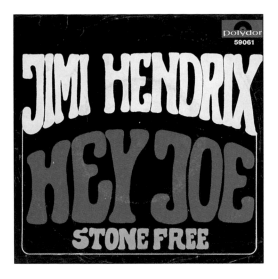

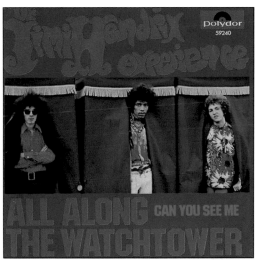

A collection of Hendrix picture sleeves.

Above: Jimi posing for photographers at London's famous Marquee Club, 24th January, 1967.

a wry face on stage during a quarter of an hour set and played the guitar with his teeth."

Audiences went wild, the momentum gaining with every show. The highlight was the tour's finale at the Paris Olympia to a capacity sellout crowd. Chandler remembers, "We worked out a great entry for him. Jimi walked out on stage playing with one hand in the air. When the audience suddenly realized that all of this great guitar sound was being played one-handed they went bananas."

Buoyed by that success, The Experience continued on to Germany where fans in Munich were witness to Jimi's first act of on-stage destruction which ironically occurred entirely by accident. As Chandler describes it, "Jimi was pulled offstage by a few over-enthusiastic fans and as he jumped back on stage he threw his guitar on before him. When he picked it up he saw it had cracked and several of the strings were broken. He just went barmy and smashed everything in sight. The German audience loved it and we decided to keep it as part of the act when there was press about or the occasion demanded it."

Sadly, Jimi's reception back in England, however, was less than enthusiastic. Despite the British underground championing his cause, the Fleet Street tabloids dubbed him the "Wild Man of Pop" and club owners wouldn't touch the band. This made it all the more vital to get a record

Penny Valentine

Release me from this noisy mob!

EXHIBITIONISTS had a field day on Saturday when the Walker Brothers' Show tour came to its conclusion at the A.B.C. Cinema, Chesterfield. Let it be said straight away, however, that the show was not nearly so dissipated as last month's Roy Orbison debacle.

Although the screaming was frenzied and occasionally reached fever pitch, it was much more under control. I have long since been a Walkers Brothers' fan following their first big chart buster "Make It Easy On Yourself," but in recent months my appreciation of their work has waned a little.

However, if anyone was in doubt about their abilities as performers they should have seen this show. It was fantastic. The only trouble was I did not hear one word of their songs due to the incredible clamouring for Scott, Gary and John. The stage presentation was extremely well supervised and for those interested in the more technical side, well worth watching.

TALENTED

and went straight up again. Next thing I knew we were in Glasgow! That was enough for me—I'd finished with flying."

★★★★★★★★★★★★★★★★★★★★★★★★★

Quote of the Month

"I saw him sitting there posing in those photographs, looking all pretty with his velvets and silks and his lacquered fingernails and I thought—'damme'—then I met him, and he was the nicest person I've ever met. I couldn't believe it! He is so nice."

Jimi Hendrix on Donovan

★★★★★★★★★★★★★★★★★★★★★★★★★

■ **Noel Redding, bass guitarist**

JIMI HENDRIX LOOKS LIKE BECOMING A LIVING LEGEND

WIND Cried Mary (Track)—As popular as Jimi Hendrix is it seems odd to suddenly issue another record so quickly after his last—as good even though it is. But ours not to reason why, and certainly the record is superb.

Let us look at this record in the light of Hendrix becoming something of a legend in his field. He wrote the song himself and sings it clearly and strongly sounding oddly like Dylan. It is very slow and more gentle than past efforts. His guitar sounds prettier, the ugly lurching has gone. It is a very careful record and one rather to listen to with satisfaction than to jump about raving to. It is a record of understatement. As such it may not have immediate commercial success but as such it is a good indication of how the man is going to expand musically.

Hendrix . . . sounds like Dylan

MY WORLD OF POP—

wild
(PARENTS AND FANS THAT IS)

about Jimi

JIMI HENDRIX EXPERIENCE . . . sometimes described by unkind critics as an unpleasant one.

YOU might think that Jimi Hendrix would appear menacingly swinging from tree tops, brandishing a spear, and yelling blood-curdling cries of " Aargh! "

For Jimi, who makes Mick Jagger look as respectable as Edward Heath and as genial as David Frost, could pass for a Hottentot on the rampage; looks as if his foot-long hair has been petrified by a thousand shock waves, and is given to playing the guitar with his teeth.

When the Jimi Hendrix Experience made its first appearance in Britain a few months ago, he was immediately dubbed "The Wild Man of Borneo," and the group was referred to as an unfortunate experience.

And yet—his first record, "Hey Joe," went straight into the top ten; his second disc, "Purple Haze," is currently No. 6, and this week his new disc, "The Wind Cries Mary" (Track) should provide him with two records simultaneously in the top ten.

polite charm that's almost olde worlde.

He stands up when you enter a room, lights all your cigarettes, and says: " Do go on," if he thinks he might be interrupting you.

Cuddly

That " ugly " image, however, doesn't worry him in the slightest.

And he says: " Some of the fans think I'm cuddly, and as long as people buy my records I'll be happy."

He could be laughing all the way to the bank.

Moan

Later this month, the wild sounds from his first LP, "Are You Experienced?" should have parents moaning for the quieter days of the Rolling Stones.

The Jimi Hendrix Experience has, it seems, filled a very necessary gap in becoming The Group They Love To Hate.

Mums and dads started liking the top pop names, but they are almost guaranteed not to dig Mr. Hendrix.

Yet Jimi Hendrix is no snarling jungle primitive.

Though the gold-braided military jacket over the black satin shirt could be taken as incongruous, Jimi off-stage behaves with a quiet

MONKEE TALK

■ **M-Day**, the Monkees' arrival date in Britain for their 3-day concert stay in early July, looks like being sooner than expected.

The group are considering filming an episode for their TV series in England in mid-June. The location is likely to be the Marquis of Bath's stately home at Longleat, Wiltshire.

If filming plans are finalised in time, Davey, Mickey, Peter and Mike could fly to England on June 15, and stay for two weeks before their concert dates at Wembley, which begin on June 30.

All tickets for their five concerts in Britain are sold out.

THE TOP 20

(Last week's position in Column 2.)

1	1	PUPPET ON A STRING—Sandie Shaw
2	3	DEDICATED TO THE ONE I LOVE— Mama's and the Papa's
3	2	SOMETHIN' STUPID—Frank and Nancy Sinatra
4	12	SILENCE IS GOLDEN—Tremeloes
5	10	THE BOAT THAT I ROW—Lulu
6	6	PURPLE HAZE—Jimi Hendrix
7	13	PICTURES OF LILY—Who
8	8	FUNNY FAMILIAR FORGOTTEN FEELINGS— Tom Jones
9	4	A LITTLE BIT ME, A LITTLE BIT YOU—Monkees
10	7	I CAN HEAR THE GRASS GROW—Move
11	9	SEVEN DRUNKEN NIGHTS—Dubliners
12	5	HA! HA! SAID THE CLOWN—Manfred Mann
13	11	I'M GONNA GET ME A GUN—Cat Stevens
14	14	BERNADETTE—Four Tops
15	15	RELEASE ME—Engelbert Humperdinck
16	16	HAPPY TOGETHER—Turtles
17	—	WATERLOO SUNSET—Kinks
18	17	HI HO SILVER LINING—Jeff Beck
19	20	SWEET SOUL MUSIC—Arthur Conley
20	26	NEW YORK MINING DISASTER 1941—Bee Gees

(By arrangement with " New Musical Express ")

---

out. On 23rd October, 1966, Jimi, Noel and Mitch went into De Lane Lea Studios to lay down their first single, *Hey Joe*. The bluesy song was a perfect vehicle for Jimi's husky voice. He was so unconfident about his singing, that he had the studio lights dimmed so that he could lay down his vocals in the comforting shadows. Ironically, his slurring rap-like delivery would become the hallmark of the recording. The production featured some elaborate overdubbing and state of the art techniques designed to highlight Jimi's quick picking and feedback harmonies.

Released on 16th December on Polydor, the single coincided with Jimi's British television debut on "Ready, Steady, Go". By New Year's Eve, *Hey Joe* charted at number thirty-eight in the national singles chart, making it into the Top Ten just three weeks later.

Jimi and The Experience, meanwhile, were breaking club records everywhere they went and attracting great attention from their peers. Paul McCartney remembers first seeing Jimi at London's trendy Bag O' Nails. "He ambled on stage, plugged in, wound up the Marshalls and started playing very loud. He was fantastic, guitar going miles away as he had a habit of doing. He was very self-effacing about his music, but then, when he picked up that guitar he was just a monster."

At their first date on 29th January, 1967, at Brian Epstein's Saville Theatre, Cream were in the audience. Eric Clapton later commented

PR 339 **TRACK RECORD**

JIMI HENDRIX EXPERIENCE

Above: Rehearsal for the German TV special 'Beat, Beat, Beat!' at the Stadthalle, Offenbach, 18th May, 1967.

Above right: A promotional postcard from Track Records (England, mid 1967).

how Jimi's blinding performance actually inspired their mega-hit *Sunshine Of Your Love*. "I don't think Jack Bruce had really taken him in before. I knew what the guy was capable of the minute I met him. It was the complete embodiment of all aspects of rock guitar rolled into one. And when Jack did see it that night, after the gig he went home and came up with the riff. It was strictly a dedication to Jimi. And then we wrote a song on top of it."

Ironically, Jimi later turned it around and used the song as his own tribute to Cream. He confided to Ginger Baker that The Experience was modeled on Cream and according to Baker's wife, Liz, "Jimi had a secret desire to join Cream."

On the heels of the success of *Hey Joe* The Experience went back into the studio to record their second single, *Purple Haze*, the revolutionary psychedelic anthem that would become Jimi's signature tune. The lyrics, written in Hendrix's dressing room of the Upper Cut Club on Boxing Day 1966, suggest a combination of many images. Interestingly, Chas Chandler refutes any suggestion that Jimi was under the influence of LSD when he wrote the tune and, in fact, no one can recall Hendrix taking acid until some six months later. However, as clarified in the magazine, *Univibes*, journalist, Keith Altham, claims that Jimi once told him: "It was

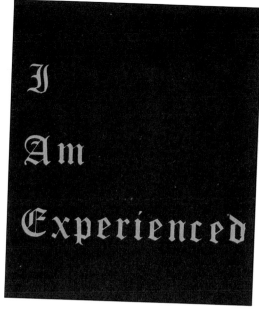

J Am Experienced

Above: A membership card of the 'Jimi Hendrix Experience Fan Club of Great Britain', 1967.

Left: After their triumph at the Monterey Pop Festival, the Jimi Hendrix Experience played for four days (20-24 June, 1967) at the Fillmore West in San Francisco, where this shot was taken.

just a straight dream I had linked upon a story I read in a science fiction magazine about a purple death ray." The images, by all accounts, were drawn from the novel, *Night of Light*, written by Philip José Farmer and published in 1957 (a short version of this novel was published in the June, 1957 edition of the American magazine *Fantasy and Science Fiction*). The story in the novel is set on the mythical planet, Dante's Joy, where, because of sunspot activity, the night sky sometimes turns violet, causing some inhabitants of the planet to go crazy. All the lyrical references in *Purple Haze* are related to this storyline, although Jimi changed the story slightly by introducing a woman into the plot as the cause of the main character's madness and confusion. In a nutshell, Jimi characterized the song, "He likes this girl so much that he doesn't know what he's in, you know. A sort of daze, I suppose."

Jimi, Noel and Mitch relaxing in Berlin, 31st August, 1967.

Opposite, main picture: Jimi usually played standard Fender guitars during concerts, but here he's playing a rarely seen Fender with tortoiseshell pickguard, at the Konserthallen-Liseberg in Gothenburg, Sweden, 3rd September, 1967.

Inset: For his blues songs Jimi mainly used a Gibson 'Flying V' guitar, also taken on 3rd September, 1967.

This new sound was so revolutionary that, according to Leon, *Purple Haze* even surprised the family. "I heard the record and said that ain't Jimi. He doesn't play music like that! Nobody dug it at first because it was so new and different. But once people started listening to the words they found there was another world out there, that unseen forces are the most powerful."

As Jimi and the band embarked on their first official tour of the UK in April (to be followed by Scandinavia) they were witness to the similar mass hysteria that had befallen The Beatles and The Stones. One bold fan did a nosedive from the balcony to land on Jimi's speakers. Another young lady tore into Jimi with a pair of scissors trying to scalp him. At the Finsbury Park Astoria Jimi's show-stopping burning guitar sent flames so high that the compère pretended he got badly burned trying to douse the blaze. He was in on the act .....

The band's success steamrolled along with the release on 5th May of their third single, *The Wind Cries Mary*. Interestingly, the delicate blues ballad, manifesting Hendrix's steady growth as a composer, was written in the wake of a furious row between Jimi and Kathy Etchingham, whose

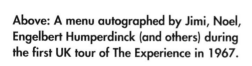

Above: A menu autographed by Jimi, Noel, Engelbert Humperdinck (and others) during the first UK tour of The Experience in 1967.

Above right: Jimi partying after he received his 'World Top Musician' award from *Melody Maker* magazine at the Europa Hotel, London, 16th September, 1967.

middle name was Mary.

May, 1967, saw the eagerly awaited release of their first album, *Are You Experienced?* The critically acclaimed work ran an extraordinary gamut from the funky *Foxy Lady* through the provocative sci-fi opus, *Third Stone From The Sun*, to the haunting title track. The eleven-song package, released in the UK, omitted the band's first three singles which were, however, included in the American version. Nonetheless, it soared in the charts, kept out of the top position only by The Beatles' revolutionary album, *Sergeant Pepper's Lonely Hearts Club Band*.

Al Hendrix recalls the first time he ever heard one of Jimi's records.

Left: Hendrix chatting to reporter Rumiko Hoshika, editor of the Japanese magazine *Music Life* at the *Melody Maker* awards in London, September, 1967.

Below: This is what Hendrix gave reporter Rumiko Hoshika for the readers of *Music Life...*

"Some hippies were living next door to us. I happened to hear this record and told my wife, 'That sounds like Jimi.' Anyway, she said, 'Well let's go next door.' I said, 'Heck no, I don't want to bother the people.' So she went over and came back with the record and they came over. They wanted to give the record to me."

On the recommendation of Paul McCartney, Hendrix was lured back to America for the three-day Monterey Pop Festival in California, which kicked off the Summer of Love. Joining such heavyweight acts as The Who, The Beach Boys, Canned Heat and Janis Joplin, this was the perfect event to launch Hendrix in America. Jimi, though, confessed to some apprehension about his home debut, "When I was in Britain I used to think about America every day. I wanted people here to see me. I also wanted to see whether we could make it back here. I was scared to go up and play in front of all those people. But you really want to turn them on. It's like a feeling of deep concern. You get very intense, that's the way I look at it."

Hendrix needn't have worried. From his rockabilly opening with *Killing Floor* to his inventive double time rendition of The Troggs' *Wild Thing*, the crowd, many tripping out on acid, roared its approval of the new

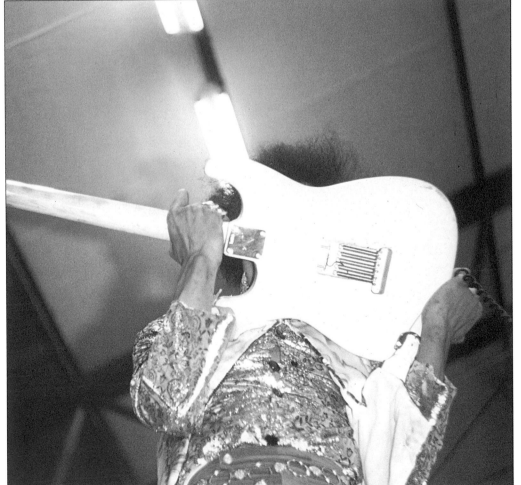

Above: An original poster for Jimi's show at the so-called 'Hippy Happy' event at Ahoy Hallen, Rotterdam, Holland, 10th November, 1967.

Left: Jimi performing at the 'Hippy Happy' event.

Opposite: Jimi in full flight on his Gibson 'Flying V' guitar - Rotterdam, November, 1967.

Advertisement for 'Christmas On Earth' happening in London, 22nd December, 1967.

king of psychedelia. In a sensational climax, Jimi set fire to his guitar, sending the crowd into a frenzy as the final chords were weirdly sustained throughout its burning. "That time I burned my guitar it was like a sacrifice," said Jimi. "You sacrifice the things you love and I love my guitar."

Los Angeles Times critic, Pete Johnson, wrote, "Their appearance at the festival was magical; the way they looked, the way they performed, the way they sounded was light years away from anything anyone had seen before. The Jimi Hendrix Experience owned the future and the audience knew it in an instant. When Jimi left the stage he graduated from rumor to legend."

In the wake of their triumph the band was booked into all the top clubs coast to coast including Bill Graham's Fillmore West and the Rheingold Festival in Central Park. However, Jimi's progress in the US was put in jeopardy by an ill-conceived tour with The Monkees, America's teenybopper heartthrobs. Despite his friendship with Monkee, Peter Tork, Hendrix was livid at the prospect. "It's so embarrassing, man, when America sends over The Monkees. Oh God! That kills me. I'm so embarrassed that America could be so stupid to make somebody like that. They could at least have done it with a group that has something to offer."

Jimi's outcry was quickly confirmed. The audience of nubile adolescents was clearly not responsive to The Experience; the reception ranged from muted to hostile and during their set The Experience had to endure the humiliation of chants of "We want the Monkees." After only eight days of gigs the band pulled out, apparently because of complaints from the conservative Daughters of the American Revolution about the indecency of Jimi's act. In fact it was revealed much later that the DAR story was an ingenious stunt dreamed up by Chas Chandler to get The Experience off The Monkees tour in such a way as to impress Jimi's loyal hippy fans. Hendrix had this to say: "Firstly, they gave us the death spot on the show, right before The Monkees were due on. The audience just screamed and yelled for The Monkees. Then some parents who brought their young kids complained that our act was vulgar. We decided it was just the wrong audience. I think they're replacing me with Mickey Mouse."

In August, Jimi's next single, *The Burning of the Midnight Lamp*, was released. Recorded at Mayfair Studios in New York City, it featured the harpsichord and was very different from anything on *Are You Experienced?* Strangely, however, it was not to achieve the chart success of Jimi's earlier singles.

By September, 1967, Jimi, Noel and Mitch were back in Olympic Studios to work on their second album, *Axis: Bold As Love*. Explains engineer, Eddie Kramer, "There were no meetings in advance and Jimi created things in a very loose fashion. He knew in his own head what he wanted and how he wanted to create. Every overdub, every backwards guitar solo was very carefully worked out in his head. I was not to know what he was going to do until he walked in the studio. I don't think anyone did."

Despite his input, Jimi complained that the final product was taken out of his hands. "The album was made over sixteen days which makes me very sad. You mix and mix and get such a beautiful sound and when it comes time to cut it, they screw it up so bad."

This follow-up to *Are You Experienced?* demonstrated a softer, more subtle approach filled with dream imagery and flashing musical colors. *Bold As Love*, the album's tour de force was a turbulent battle of passions, once again heavily laced with American Indian imagery. "Like the axis of the earth, you know," Hendrix explained. "If it changes, well it changes the whole face of the Earth like every few thousand years. It's like love in a human being; if he really falls deep enough it will change him. It might change his whole life. So both of them really go together."

But even as this second album, which would receive universal rave reviews, was released, Jimi was dissatisfied as he contemplated the bigger picture. "You can only freak out when you feel like it. I used to feel like freaking out a lot, but man, if I did it all the time I'd be dead two years ago. I know we'll have to change some way, but I don't know how to do it. I suppose this staleness will finish us in the end."

Even as Jimi was formulating another challenge, he was already becoming a victim of his own success. On 14th November, 1967, The Experience kicked off its second UK tour at the Royal Albert Hall in a monster concert which also included Pink Floyd, The Move and the Nice. Backstage the boys could hear frenzied screams throughout the packed house. Chas Chandler remembers: "Noel and Mitch were shaking like leaves and even Jimi was petrified to go on stage. They realized that they were part of something bigger than themselves and I had to get a bottle of Scotch to restore some courage all around."On the stage of the Albert Hall it truly dawned on Jimi and The Experience: they were now full fledged superstars.

"Jimi used to give away a lot of things. A lot of people owe him money out there. I mean they'd just be bugging him and so on."
Al Hendrix

CHAPTER FOUR

ROOM FULL OF MIRRORS: STARDOM

"A couple of years ago all I wanted was to be heard. 'Let me in' was the thing. Now I'm trying to figure out the *wisest* way to be heard."

Jimi Hendrix

O N 4TH JANUARY, 1968, The Experience was starting a Scandinavian tour in Gothenburg, Sweden. Claiming someone had spiked his drink Jimi went on a rampage in Mitch Mitchell's hotel room the previous night, destroying literally every bit of furniture and cutting his hand severely after smashing it through a window. It finally took four of Gothenburg's policemen to place the cuffs on him and haul him off to jail, where he was subsequently charged with criminal damage.

Recounts Chandler, "I think Noel hit Jimi and Jimi laid out two cops and tried to jump out of the window. He had been in hospital to have stitches for two gashes in his hands. Then they put him in a cell. He was absolutely out of his mind."

A month later Jimi and the band kicked off an American tour at Bill Graham's Winterland, before heading off on a western leg that included Jimi's Seattle homecoming and his first meeting with his father in seven years. He had earlier told a journalist in Berlin, "I'm scared to go home. My father is a very strict man. He would straight away grab hold of me, tear my clothes off and cut my hair."

Happily, the return of the prodigal son resulted in a warm family reunion. By this time Al had remarried and adopted his wife's young daughter, Janie, whom Jimi instantly adored. "We were happy for once," admitted Jimi. "I told my dad, I've got a six-year-old sister who I'd never seen, a lovely little girl."

Beamed Mr. Hendrix, "I was sure proud of him. During the show the family was right down there in the front row, smiling up at him. I had to pinch myself several times; is that really our Jimi up there?"

As The Experience played to more capacity crowds and rave reviews, a series of bizarre incidents unfolded: a near fatal brush with sniper fire in Detroit, riotous fans wreaking havoc on the Cleveland Music Hall and Jimi's infamous encounter with the Plaster Casters in Chicago which captured the legendary Hendrix "rig", a sculpture one writer compared with

Opposite: Lift off! The Jimi Hendrix Experience arrive at the Hotel Opalen, Gothenburg, 3rd January, 1968. Later that night, after being spiked, Jimi smashed up Mitch Mitchell's room in the hotel.

the Venus de Milo. "More like the Leaning Tower of Pisa," Hendrix wryly remarked.

The highlight of absolute absurdity, though, occurred in Montreal where zealous fans crashed the stage and began making off with guitars, equipment, anything they could get hold of. During a concert in Canada Jim Morrison staggered up to the front of the stage shouting, "Hey Jimi! Let me come up and sing, man, and we'll do this fuckin' shit together!"

"That's okay, man, I can handle it," Jimi replied kindly.

To which an indignant Morrison screeched, "Hey, do you know who I am?, I'm Jim Morrison of The Doors!"

Jimi retorted, "I know who you are, and I'm Jimi Hendrix."

Life on the road contained more than its share of the absurd. One part of the Hendrix myth that truly lived up to the legend, however, was Jimi's seemingly endless succession of women. Brother Leon remembers a visit to Jimi's hotel would usually feature a harem of fifteen or so young lovelies, all vying for Jimi's intimate attention. "Many times I would just be falling asleep from some all night orgy and I would hear a gentle knock on my door." Hendrix recalled. "I'd stagger to the door naked, peep out and there would be some cute little thing standing there who would ask if she could come in. Most of the time I'd say yes."

Ginger Baker, recalls an orgy with a trio of stunning ladies, including a popular singer's former wife: "They kept saying, Jim's coming back soon and I finally asked them, who's this Jim you're on about? They said, "Jimi Hendrix" and I panicked, thinking Jimi's going to kill me when he finds out I've been with his girls! Thankfully, I met him a few days later in a club and he draped his arm around me, smiling. He was very cool about it."

The trio's other extracurricular activities were also steadily getting out of hand. Aside from smoking a lot of dope, everyone in the band was tripping on LSD and another hallucinogen, DMT. Jimi also indulged in the occasional snort of cocaine. Noel was usually popping amyl nitrate capsules, while Mitch carried an airline bag with compartments for what he dubbed sleepers (barbiturates), leapers (amphetamines) and creepers (tranquilizers). Interestingly, a lot of this stuff was obtained legally, on a doctor's prescription!

Mitch recalls an incident when someone had given the band what they believed to be a pick-me-up to combat fatigue one night just before they took to the stage: "We got up to play and I looked up and saw the guy who gave us the powder in a tower about twenty-five feet above the stage. Suddenly I was on the same level as him, looking down at this empty shell playing the drums. I looked across and there's Jimi up there with me and we kind of look at each other and nod, 'Gig going okay, so far?' Obviously, the powder wasn't what we thought."

April of 1968 found the band in Newark, New Jersey in the wake of the Martin Luther King assassination. Jimi walked out on stage and told the crowd, "This is for a friend of mine" and proceeded to drop his normal set in favor of a moving improvisation that left many in the audience in tears. He followed it up with a $5,000 donation to the Martin Luther King Foundation in June.

The second Newark concert, however, had to be cancelled because of

Opposite: Lorensberg Cirkus, Gothenburg, 4th January, 1968.

Inset: Jimi playing at Lorensberg Cirkus with a bandaged right hand (from his 'smashing experience' at Hotel Opalen).

Above: Taking time out to write some lyrics at the Esso Motor Hotel while waiting for his courtcase to come up, Gothenburg, mid January, 1968.

Right: A free man again! Jimi leaving Gothenburg's Municipal Court in a taxi, 16th January, 1968.

riots which had been sparked off by the King assassination. Even at the first concert many ticket holders opted for the safety of their homes, and the auditorium was far from full. It must be remembered that Hendrix appealed to a largely white audience.

Al Hendrix recalls his son's lifelong commitment to civil rights. "They used to sit in the area of the theatre where blacks weren't allowed. They'd get arrested and the guy at the club they were playing would have to come and get them out. He used to take the bail out of their wages. Jimi would tell me, 'Well, I'm only doing what I think you ought to.' Jimi was always involved with those kinds of issues."

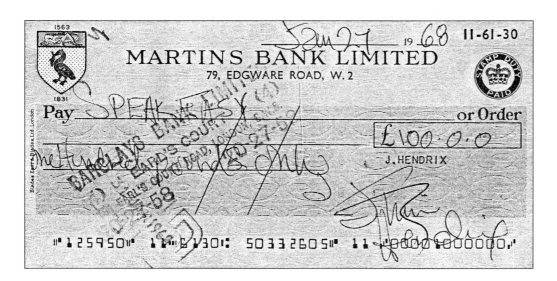

Left: Collectable Hendrix. Jimi settles his Speakeasy club bill in London.

DATE	DEBIT		CREDIT	BALANCE
23 JAN 68	BALANCE FWD			8. 17. 6 CR
24 JAN 68	946.	5. 0. 0		3. 17. 6 CR
25 JAN 68	SDY	15, 15. 0		11. 17. 6 DR
27 JAN 68	948.	200. 0. 0		211. 17. 6 CR
31 JAN 68	959.	35. 0. 0		
	950.	100. 0. 0		
	947.	20. 0. 0		366. 17. 6 CR
1 FEB 68			C.T 1,000. 0. 0	
	949.	61. 0. 0		572. 2. 6 CR
14 FEB 68	214.	88. 0. 0		484. 2. 6 CR
27 FEB 68	COM	1. 10. 0		
	INT	13. 2		481. 19. 4 CR

IN ACCOUNT WITH
MARTINS BANK LIMITED
79 EDGWARE ROAD
LONDON. W 2

JIMI HENDRIX ESQ

COM. COMMISSION
CQB. CHEQUE BOOK
CSH. CASH AND/OR CHEQUES
C.T. CREDIT TRANSFER
(THIRD PARTY CREDIT)

DIV. DIVIDEND
INT. INTEREST
SAL. SALARY
SDY. SUNDRY

S.O. STANDING ORDER
SUP. SUPPLEMENTARY LIST AS ENCLOSED
TFR. TRANSFER TO OR FROM
ANOTHER ACCOUNT

302N

CHEQUES ARE DESIGNATED BY THE LAST THREE FIGURES OF THEIR SERIAL NUMBERS

Michael Jeffery Management, Inc.
27 East 37th Street
New York, New York 10016
(212) 689-0810

23rd November, 1969.

Received from Gerry Stickells the sum of $2,500. 00.
cash for personal use.

Signed: Jimi Hendrix.

Left: Apparently, Jimi's claims that he never made the money he should have done were justified. Witness this 1968 bank statement.

Above: Although Jimi did seem to do somewhat better in 1969...

Two weeks on, following a well deserved rest, Jimi and the band were laying down tracks for the haunting double album, *Electric Ladyland* at Jimi's favorite studio, New York's sophisticated Record Plant. The ambitious project signaled a marked change in Hendrix's style and heralded the beginnings of a serious split in his creative and personal relationships with Mitch and Noel.

Frustrated by his lack of control over the *Axis* album, Hendrix was eager to flex his artistic muscle, refusing to take advice and spending an entire week to remix a single song some three hundred times. Notes Chandler, "He wasn't listening anymore. He wanted to go over and over

Above: Poster for a concert at the Sacramento State College, California, 8th February 1968.

Right: Jimi's first visit back to Seattle as an international star - with Al and stepsister Janie, backstage at the Center Arena, 12th February 1968.

songs he'd often gotten on the first take. I just couldn't communicate with him. I felt like an alien."

Echoes Redding, "Things had to be done Jimi's way or no way and Jimi's way was getting more and more unproductive. Nothing was happening, the recording process got stretched out into marathon twiddling sessions. Chas was getting fed up. He had successfully produced the first two albums, but now found himself stymied by Jimi's demands for control."

The studio sessions soon developed the aspect of a sideshow, with dozens of hangers-on regularly turning up. Jimi was to comment later that *Electric Ladyland* was dedicated to groupies everywhere. "Some groupies know more about music than the guys. Some people call them groupies, but I prefer the term Electric Ladies. My whole *Electric Ladyland* album is about them."

To further complicate matters, Jimi found an unexpected acid buddy in Michael Jeffery, Chas Chandler's former personal manager and now his partner in the management of The Experience. Jeffery's involvement in Jimi's drug use made it even more difficult for Chandler to control or even to limit it. "Drugs were getting in the way of his brain, mainly acid. He was dropping everyday; it was madness, it had to stop."

Even Jimi's father understood the toll that Hendrix's drug use was having on him. "He used to take something on account of they had to keep going so much. He'd be working two or three jobs and he would take

amphetamines and I'd say, 'Dog gone, you're going to fall out sometime if you keep working around the clock like that.' Jimi was on the road all the time, it was just, go, go, go. The time I saw him I said, 'I could put my hand around your waist.'" He was convinced that Jimi was harming himself and that Jeffery was not working in his best interests.

Finally, Chandler had had enough. He sold his half interest in Hendrix to Jeffery for $300,000 and, almost exactly two years after he had first brought Jimi to London, he got out. For Jimi, the move would ultimately prove disastrous. Chandler had been Hendrix's barometer and confidant, a trusted advisor both musically and personally. A true friend who kept outside pressures at bay. As a businessman, Jeffery was primarily interested in making money, not in his client's welfare, artistic or otherwise. As Leon Hendrix once said, "He had no vision."

Following Chandler's departure, Jimi took over the reins of the album. Enlisting musicians like Traffic's Steve Winwood, bassist Jack Casady from Jefferson Airplane and drummer Buddy Miles, who had worked with Mike Bloomfield in Electric Flag. Mitchell and Redding were pushed into the background. Noel in particular, was hurt by Jimi's dismissal of his song, *Little Miss Strange*, the only

Above: It's a family affair! Field International Airport, Seattle, 12th February, 1968.
Left to right: Janie Hendrix (just a bit of her), unknown, Al Hendrix, Ayako 'June' Hendrix (Jimi's stepmother), Jimi, Pat MacDonald (local reporter), Freddie Mae Gautier and Leon Hendrix.

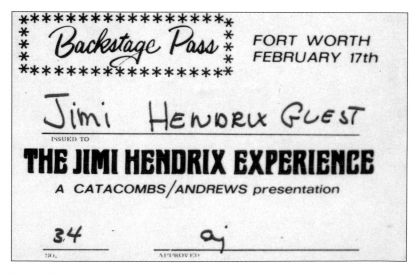

A backstage pass for an Experience concert in Fort Worth, Texas, 17th February, 1968.

Above: Poster for two concerts in Zürich, Switzerland, 30th and 31st May, 1968.

Right: Jimi spent most of 1968 touring and recording in the USA, hence this plea published in the *Disc and Music Echo* issue of 25th May, 1968.

Remember your British fans, Jimi

WHEN WILL Jimi Hendrix be back in the British pop scene? Surely he must realise that thousands of his fans over here in England are very upset about his long stay in America. He has even released records in the States, and yet here we haven't even heard anything about a new single. Don't forget your friends in England, Jimi. Show everybody how great you are.— MISS C. RICKETTS, 3 Domville Drive, Woodchurch Estate, Birkenhead, Cheshire.

● Why have the Yardbirds deserted Britain? In the past year we have had one single issued and two promised singles that never appeared—no albums —no TV and virtually no radio or live appearances. Britain has not forgotten the group who gave us "For Your Love", "Still I'm Sad" and "Shapes Of Things," so don't forget us, Yardbirds, come back from America and show us where it's really at! —NICK LAMBERT, 14 Boundary Gardens, Newcastle-upon-Tyne 7.

Redding composition to make the album.

"To get back at Hendrix, I would purposely play out of tune," Noel revealed. "I knew Jimi was going to play over it anyway."

Despite the turmoil on *Electric Ladyland*, the final product was critically acclaimed, demonstrating a wide range of styles from the powerful *Voodoo Chile*, arguably the finest modern interpretation of Delta blues, to the jazz-inspired R&B boogie, *Crosstown Traffic* to the highly original *1983, Moon Turn the Tides*, and *The Gods Made Love* which feature a panorama of freaky sounds and special effects that Hendrix once termed 'sound painting'.

The album, released in October, 1968, also included Hendrix's smash hit single in Bob Dylan's *All Along The Watchtower*. Its cryptic, rather obscure and secretive lyrics married beautifully to Jimi's guitar hallmark,

the eloquent talking wah-wah which lifted the song to another artistic realm. Said Jimi: "In the early days I used to ask my producer to drown my voice in the backing track, I thought it was so bad. But I was basing my assessment of my voice on the wrong things. Now I base my singing on real feelings and true thoughts. I learned that from Dylan. I felt like *Watchtower* was something I had written, but could never get together. I often feel like that about Dylan generally."

Dylan himself readily concurred. "It's not a wonder to me that he recorded my songs, but rather that he recorded so few because they were all *his*."

Immediately following the release of this ambitious album, which appeared in a controversial sleeve showing Jimi surrounded by naked women, the band went to perform in the USA. "This was the moment when we stopped making music and started doing time," said Redding. Paradoxically, The Experience were at the very height of their popularity, virtually the biggest act in rock, often taking in $100,000 or more per show. In addition, Jimi had been voted best musician by virtually every trade magazine. Now playing almost exclusively in stadiums and large arenas, mob hysteria took over, with fans clamoring to see the heralded 'Wild Man of Pop' perform his well known and outrageous stage exploits.

"I'm not a damn clown. I'm not a monkey on a stick!" Jimi would often hiss, cursing to the audience and storming off.

Above left: Jimi playing an original 1954/58 Gibson 'Les Paul' Custom guitar in Zürich, Switzerland, 31st May, 1968.

Above: Unknown venue, possibly in California, August, 1968.

Another shot from the family album. Left to right: Leon, Al, Jimi and his stepsister Janie. Seattle, 6th September, 1968.

An original press release.

Adds Kathy Etchingham, "He started to hate his image. He would sit at the end of the bed in tears trying to explain how he felt, how he was fed up with his stage act and what people expected of him."

Clearly, Hendrix was changing direction. Shedding the stolid trio format, guest musicians would frequently sit in with the band and by their three October, 1968 dates at San Francisco's Winterland, Jimi was experimenting with looser, free flow jams.

By the tour's end, a split was inevitable and imminent. Mitchell was eager to return to England where he had session work awaiting him, while Redding had already formed his own band, Fat Mattress. In November Hendrix announced to the press, "Mitch and Noel want to get their own thing going, producing and managing other artists, so very soon, probably in the New Year, we'll be breaking up the group, apart from select dates."

Left: The Jimi Hendrix Experience in Seattle, 6th September, 1968.

The UK cover for the double album *Electric Ladyland* put together by Track Records - Jimi wasn't consulted and hated the design...

As 1969 dawned, however, unsettling outside forces were closing in on Jimi. Business deals and financial power plays gave Michael Jeffery a legal strangle-hold on Hendrix. The Experience was his main source of income and he was determined to squeeze as much as he could out of the successful formula. "Pop slavery," Jimi fired back in an obvious reference to Jeffery. "That's the trouble with this business. People can see where they can make fast bread and they have you up there being a slave to the public. They keep you doing the same thing until you're exhausted."

In pursuit of further profit Jeffery managed to get The Experience back on stage in February at London's Royal Albert Hall. Remembers Chandler, "That was a lousy show, among the worst I had ever seen Jimi play. And it wasn't his fault, it was Mitch and Noel's. Mitchell's timing was totally off, like he was out of his brain and Redding was just trying to show how awkward he could be. If I had been in charge they would have been sacked the next day." Tapes of the show, however, reveal that this only referred to a few songs; the rest were fine and up to The Experience's normal standard.

Rheinhalle, Düsseldorf, Germany,
12th January, 1969 (second show).

During the subsequent American tour the band played through a myriad of riots to hostile, stoned out crowds, with Jimi increasingly becoming the subject of racist taunts. "People call me the Black Elvis and say I play white music for white people," he countered. "It's a kind of 'Let's strip him naked and hang him from a tall tree attitude.' Music is universal, there is no *white* rock or *black* rock. I feel sorry for the minorities, but I don't feel part of one. Music is far stronger than politics or even race. The answer lies within the music."

Problems escalated. Arriving in Canada on 3rd May, a routine customs check turned up several small envelopes of heroin in Jimi's luggage. Despite persistent tabloid fodder to the contrary, Hendrix was definitely not a heroin user and claimed vehemently that he'd been set up.

The unsavory episode cast a shadow over the remainder of the tour, which culminated on 29th June at the Denver Pop Festival. It was a frenzied scene of rampant drug dealing, gate crashing and rioting throughout the stadium, which Denver police, armed with tear gas, were scarcely able to contain. In the middle of the bedlam Jimi, Mitch and Noel were escorted off stage in a U-Haul truck.

For Redding this latest escapade proved one bitter experience too

many. The clincher had been speculation that Hendrix would be expanding the trio, a development Jimi never saw fit to discuss with his bassist. "That was the last straw," said Noel. "It did my head in. I was uneasy enough about our future, but this just blew me away. I went up to Jimi, told him goodbye and caught the next plane to London." The Jimi Hendrix Experience had performed their final concert together.

Going into seclusion following the tour, Hendrix emerged with renewed spirits. He had moved to Woodstock, New York with a group of musicians, including old pals Billy Cox and Larry Lee, where he had conceived the latest Hendrix invention, something he called 'Electric Church Music'.

Jimi explained it this way, "It's more than music. It's like church, like a foundation for the potentially lost. We're making music into a new kind of Bible, a Bible you can carry in your hearts. When I get up on stage and sing, that's my whole life. That's my religion. I am electric religion."

The debut of the new band proved an auspicious one, performing at the largest commune in rock history, the three-day Woodstock Music and Arts Fair in August, 1969. The festival organizers, in recognition of his unique status, selected Hendrix to wrap up the historic event. Jimi was

Mitch and Jimi arrive at Berlin Airport, 23rd January, 1969.

Opposite top: Tuning-up time at Lorensberg Cirkus, Gothenburg, 8th January, 1969.

HAROLD DAVISON PRESENTS
AN EVENING WITH

Jimi Hendrix Experience

THE SOFT MACHINE
MASON, CAPALDI
WOOD & FROG
LONDON · ROYAL ALBERT HALL
TUESDAY, 18 FEB., at 7.30 p.m.
TICKETS: 3/6, 7/6, 10/6, 13/6, 16/6, 21/-
Available from ROYAL ALBERT HALL BOX
OFFICE (589 8212) and HAROLD DAVISON
LTD., REGENT HOUSE, 235-241 REGENT
STREET, LONDON, W.1

*Please send stamped addressed envelope with
postal applications*

Opposite: Rehearsals at the Royal Albert Hall, London, 18th February, 1969.

Opposite inset: Advertisement for Jimi's concert on 18th February, 1969, in London. The gig instantly sold out, so a second concert was added, which took place six days later.

Left: Afternoon rehearsals at the Royal Albert Hall, London, 24th February, 1969.

Overleaf: Royal Albert Hall, London, 24th February, 1969.

Above: A hard to find poster showing Jimi during a USA performance in spring 1969.

Above left: Autograph hunters outside the courtroom of the Old City Hall in Toronto, Canada, 5th May, 1969, where Jimi faced a charge of illegal possession of narcotics.

Above: A snapshot taken by a fan on 11th May, 1969 at the Fairgrounds Coliseum, Indianapolis, Indiana.

Left: Jimi and Noel arrive at Seattle Airport, 23rd May, 1969.

Top: 'Sunshine' music provided by the Experience during a pop festival at the Santa Clare County Fairgrounds, San Jose, California, 25th May, 1969.

Above: Another groovy concert poster, this time for Seattle, 23rd May, 1969.

backed by Billy Cox, Larry Lee on rhythm guitar, Juma Sultan and Jerry Velez (both on percussion) and Mitch Mitchell. The set, which included *Red House and Purple Haze*, was capped by Jimi's searing seven-minute epiphany of *The Star Spangled Banner*, a fitting and memorable close.

 Incredibly, in October Jimi was kidnapped in New York City. Unidentified thugs (possibly from the Mafia) whisked him upstate. Michael Jeffery was incensed by the kidnapping, and, despite the fact that Hendrix called to say he was being well treated and would be back in a couple of days, Jeffery insisted on hiring some muscle to overpower the kidnappers at their safe house near Woodstock to rescue the guitarist. The whole bizarre event remains a mystery, but it must prompt the question of whether it was a publicity stunt devised by Michael Jeffery.

 "He was really scared because he thought that either they wanted to hurt him really badly or kill him," remembers Monika Dannemann, Jimi's German girlfriend at the time. "But after a time, he said, 'It's strange, they didn't do anything to hurt me and they didn't really say what they wanted.' After a day or so, a couple of people hired by his management freed him. Jimi told me that Michael Jeffery told him if they hadn't rescued him, he would be dead and that he should be very grateful. But Jimi

WOODSTOCK
MUSIC & ART FAIR
PRESENTS AN
AQUARIAN EXPOSITION
IN WHITE LAKE, N.Y.

Jimi Hendrix

★ ★ ★

3 Days of
Peace & Music
AUGUST 1969

★ ★ ★

Grateful Dead   **Janis Joplin**

Music Starts at 4:00pm on Fri. and 1:00pm Sat. & Sun.

Friday 15th	Saturday 16th	Sunday 17th
Joan Baez	Canned Heat	The Band
Arlo Guthrie	Creedence Clearwater	Jeff Beck Group
Richie Havens	Grateful Dead	Blood, Sweat & Tears
Sly and The Family Stone	Janis Joplin	Joe Cocker
Tim Hardin	Jefferson Airplane	Crosby Stills & Nash
Nick Benes	Santana	Jimi Hendrix
Sweetwater	The Who	Iron Butterfly
	Jack Harrison	Ten Years After
		Jonny Winter

★ ★ ★ ★ ★ ★

HUNDRED OF ACRES TO ROAM ON
Ticket Prices, One Day $7.00
Two Days $13.00. Three Days $18.00

Above: *The Electric Church: A Visual Experience* was sold at Experience concerts in the USA during 1969.

Top and opposite: A perfect summer's night on 139th Street in Harlem. A free show for the 'United Block Association' on 5th September, 1969.

started to think it strange how they just came in and freed him. He figured that the whole thing was a set-up by his management."

Lending some credence to the Mafia angle, however, was the mob's uneasiness about the construction of Jimi's Electric Lady Studios on Manhattan's Eighth Street, bordering Little Italy, a Mafia dominated neighbourhood. The project, a long time dream of Jimi and engineer, Eddie Kramer, had already attracted the attention of the FBI, and the mob was concerned that Hendrix would attract a heavy drug scene and make it too hot for them to run their business as usual.

Meanwhile, as the year rolled on, Hendrix's new band, the Band of Gypsys, which included Buddy Miles and Billy Cox, began to rehearse for two upcoming shows at Bill Graham's Fillmore East, in New York, due to take place on 31st December, 1969 and 1st January, 1970. The gigs, recorded live, were received with the kind of critical attention generally reserved for great classical artists. Graham called it "the most brilliant, emotional display of virtuoso electric guitar playing I have ever heard."

Unfortunately, disaster struck on 28th January during the Gypsys' next gig at Madison Square Garden to benefit the Vietnam Moratorium Committee. Someone passed Jimi some bad acid and he was clearly in

Jimi and actor Robert Young appear on 'The Dick Cavett Show' on ABC TV, New York City, 9th September, 1969.

no state to go on. Johnny Winter recalls: "When I saw him backstage it gave me the chills. It was the most horrible thing I'd ever seen. He came in with this entourage of people and it was like he was already dead. He didn't move until it was time for the show."

It was a show Hendrix should clearly never have given. Following two disjointed, spaced out attempts at playing, Jimi told the audience, "I'm sorry, but we just can't get it together," and left the stage. While some contend it was a stranger who gave Hendrix the bad acid, Buddy Miles swears it was none other than Michael Jeffery himself who "gave Jimi a couple of tabs that brought him to his knees and cramped up his stomach. Jeffery wanted to make us look bad."

The opportunistic Jeffery fired Miles a few days later, which conveniently opened the way to re-form the old Experience. A press conference was hurriedly arranged to announce that Redding and Mitchell were back on board. Shortly afterwards, however, Jimi changed his mind and

retained Billy Cox on bass.

While he recalled Mitchell, he was not prepared to have Redding in his band. "I had always planned to change bass players," asserted Hendrix. "Noel is definitely out. The Experience is a ghost now, it's dead like yesterday's flowers."

Jimi had taken a stand and he was serving notice that it was time to do things his way. But his time was about to run out.

"I know that the blacks didn't understand his music. That kind of surprised him, but he had a bigger white following than a black one."
Al Hendrix

Jimi and friends (left: Lynn Bailey, right: Jeanette Jacobs) celebrate following his acquittal at the Toronto Court House on 10th December, 1969. Jimi's sober suit was specially made for the occasion!

CHAPTER FIVE

THE STORY OF LIFE: MISSION ACCOMPLISHED

"It's funny the way people love the dead. Once you're dead you are made for life. You have to die before they think you're worth anything."
Jimi Hendrix

THE SPRING 'CRY OF LOVE' TOUR was launched against a background of difficult personal problems for Jimi. Several lawsuits tied up his cash flow and he was also in debt because of over-budget costs on his Electric Lady Studios. On top of that, glandular troubles left him tired and ill for most of the tour. It is possible that Hendrix may have been suffering from what we now call Chronic Fatigue Syndrome or Chronic Infectious Mononucleosis. This would also explain a lot of Hendrix's well documented anxiety and depression at this time. At this point, Jimi had grown mistrustful of nearly everyone around him.

As a result, the thirty-one American dates revealed an uninspired Hendrix, trapped in a stale format before an audience who clearly wanted to keep him from moving on. New material like *Message To Love* and Ezy Ryder drew only a lukewarm reception at best. However, these new songs had not been released at that stage, so they were not familiar to the concert fans. At one point when the restless crowds called out for *Hey Joe*, Jimi shot back, "Hey, I'm no jukebox!"

Added Mitch, "I have to say, that most of the gigs were unmemorable, the same old places yet again. It was really starting to lose its rock'n'roll flavor. This was like the old band, but much less exciting."

The exceptions were two concerts on 30th May, 1970 at the three hundred seat Berkeley Community Theater, which took place in the middle of tense anti-Vietnam War riots. While angry fans scaled the roof looking for a way in, the atmosphere on stage was vintage Hendrix, sizzling with the old energy while demonstrating his maturing virtuosity. No longer simply a raw talent attacking the guitar, his Stratocaster had become a conduit for a wider range of expression of piercing special effects and subtle nuances. The masterful performance shines through on the now classic, *Jimi Plays Berkeley* video.

The same could not be said, however, for the so-called occult documentary, *Rainbow Bridge* filmed on the lush Hawaiian isle of Maui.

Opposite: On stage, May 1970, USA.

BILL GRAHAM PRESENTS

BERKELEY COMMUNITY THEATRE

FRIDAY, MAY 29
8:00 P.M.

JAMES TAYLOR
THE PENTANGLE

SATURDAY, MAY 30

TWO SHOWS
7:30 & 10 P.M.

JIMI HENDRIX
EXPERIENCE
WITH
MITCH MITCHELL & BILLY COX

A flyer for two terrific shows at the Berkeley Community Theatre.

Opposite: Jimi Hendrix as we remember him best, the raving good time performer. Temple University Stadium, Philadelphia, Pennsylvania, 16th May, 1970.

Hyped as a "Living, breathing piece of late sixties, southern California, acid trip memorabilia," even the spectacular backdrop of volcanic craters couldn't save what Mitch Mitchell described as, "The worst film I've ever seen, a complete bloody shambles."

A few days previously Jimi had played his last gig in Seattle on 26th July in the middle of the pouring rain. Hendrix, in good form, played before 9,000 soaked and disgruntled fans.

Leaving the Seattle experience behind, Hendrix found renewed enthusiasm in his spanking new million dollar baby, Electric Lady Studios in New York City. An acoustic marvel boasting a controlled theatrical lighting system, film projection suite and floating ceilings, the facility provided one of the first fully functional sixteen track recorders. That summer of 1970 Jimi started work with Billy Cox and Mitch on the production of his most ambitious project yet for the planned double album, *First Rays of the New Rising Sun*. From the funky *Dolly Dagger* - a sardonic swipe at occasional companion Devon Wilson - to the delicate tapestry of *Angel*, perhaps his finest ballad ever, Hendrix was steadily conquering new ground. He even recorded several instrumentals that featured classical flamenco and concerto-type movements.

The exhausting sessions, though, left no time for rest. Mike Jeffery had arranged a brief European tour, kicked off by the Isle of Wight Festival, remembered today as the last great fling of the British counter-culture. Suffering from severe fatigue and depression and plagued by stubborn technical problems Jimi stumbled badly, at times both playing and singing out of tune.

Later that evening (30th August, 1970) singer, Richie Havens, recalls an eerie encounter with Hendrix on a foggy country road near the festival. "Hey, man what's happening?" he called out to Jimi.

"Ah man, it's just so frustrating," Hendrix complained, stopping to lean against a fence post. "It's Jeffery, you know. I don't trust him. He's trying to keep me in this fuckin' little box, forcing me to play the same old shit. It's a drag man."

Hendrix was clearly desperately discouraged and unhappy.

"That was the last time I ever saw him," recalls Havens.

Meanwhile, death seemed to be a favorite topic in Hendrix's recent interviews with reporters. In July he commented, "The next time I go back to Seattle it will be in a pine box," and while on this tour he told journalist Anne Bjørnal, "I've been dead for a long time. I don't think I will live to see twenty-eight."

Moving on to Sweden and Denmark, where Jimi enjoyed god-like status, things temporarily got back on track. The attentive, knowledgeable audience allowed him to indulge his more progressive material and as a result he performed several sparkling shows.

Then, just as suddenly, it all went wrong again. Germany's Isle of Fehmarn so-called Love and Peace Festival was anything but. In the midst of a howling gale, German Hell's Angels went berserk, robbing the box office at gunpoint, going on a shooting spree and inciting a terrifying riot. Confused fans booed and shouted, "Yankee go home!" sending the band fleeing from the stage. Little did Jimi know, it was the last real concert he would ever play.

Jimi plays Berkeley, 30th May, 1970.

To make matters worse, the normally quiet and stable Billy Cox had apparently been slipped some bad acid in Sweden and erupted into a violent, uncontrollable state of manic paranoia. "We're not going to get off this island alive! It's going to be taken over by the Nazis!" he rambled to Mitch and Jimi.

Unable to be subdued, Cox was rushed to hospital where he was administered a heavy and much needed dose of Thorazine. His old friend now reduced to a catatonic mess, Hendrix arranged for Billy to be confined in a London apartment, fearing that he might be institutionalized. The remainder of the tour was abruptly cancelled. Jimi Hendrix would never play a proper concert again.

By mid-September Hendrix was jamming at Ronnie Scott's, a popular London jazz club, while blocking out studio time at Electric Lady for his scheduled return to New York. "I want a big band full of competent musicians I can conduct and write for," Hendrix commented at the time. "Strauss and Wagner are going to form the background of my music. Floating in the sky above it all will be the blues."

Jimi was also keeping steady company with Monika Dannemann, a

Above: A scene from the movie *Rainbow Bridge*, Hawaii, 30th July, 1970.

Left: The Atlanta Pop Festival, where Jimi Hendrix performed on 4th July, 1970.

blonde German ice skating instructor and artist. Sweet and innocent, from a well-to-do Düsseldorf family, she was the very antithesis of the streetwise Devon Wilson. Rumor had it that she and Jimi had recently become engaged. Hendrix may have been ready to settle down.

"He used to say, 'Oh no!' he wouldn't even think about getting married," Mr. Hendrix remembers. "But the last time he was here and he mentioned it to me. We sat down and talked and he said, 'Daddy, I've been thinking seriously about getting married and settling down.' I said, 'That's strange coming from you.' But he was getting older, becoming more settled...."

"I remember telling him, 'Well, in your position all the gals know who you are. That's the way it goes with all famous people unless you got somebody in particular already picked out. I mean, you'll find so many applicants, they'll just stand there waiting.' Oh wow!"

In an interview Monika Dannemann later spoke about Jimi's wedding plans. "Jimi talked of marriage very early on in our relationship. He caught me by surprise there. That was in March, 1969. We were somewhere in London and he went into a jewelry shop and bought two rings, snake rings they were. And in the evening we went to the Speakeasy and he declared to everybody that we were engaged. He went everywhere showing everybody the rings. He was so proud and happy. At this time though, I didn't even think about it, because we had just met one and a half months before."

"He immediately started to make plans that we were getting married in October. He already told his father that we were getting married. He asked me to get a house in the country because he wanted to come live in England. Finally, I didn't buy a house because he wanted it for our main home and I wanted to choose it with him. So I got a very beautiful flat in London for us, but because things were still so heavy in America, he checked into a hotel. Nobody knew where he was and everybody would have to approach him from the hotel. Only in the last week did people somehow find out where we were."

Ginger Baker remembers how Hendrix would sometimes visit his own family in London: "Off stage Jimi was very gentle and soft-spoken. He was completely mesmerized by my family, collecting all the kids and sitting them on his lap. As I sat there observing him, it occurred to me how we each seemed to have what the other wanted. I had this fantasy about having all of Jimi's women and he secretly desired a home and family."

But it was never to be. On the night of 17th September, 1970, Jimi returned after a party to Monika Dannemann's flat in Lansdowne Crescent in Ladbroke Grove. At some point during the night he took a total of nine sleeping tablets. The following morning, after going out to buy cigarettes, Monika found that Hendrix had vomited in his sleep. Unable to rouse him she eventually called an ambulance. By the time the ambulance arrived at the hospital, just before noon, the paramedics realised that they were too late. The staff at St. Mary Abbott's Hospital were also unable to revive Jimi. The official cause of death was inhalation of vomit due to acute barbitu-

Opposite: James Marshall Hendrix: Voodoo Child. A dramatic action shot from Hawaii, 30th July, 1970.

A rare poster advertising Jimi's concert in Honolulu on 1st August, 1970. As it turned out, this was Jimi's last official concert in North America.

rate intoxication. Just as he had predicted, Jimi Hendrix had not lived to see his twenty-eighth birthday.

The news was released to a stunned world. Ginger Baker recalls trying to locate Hendrix that fateful night along with Mitch Mitchell and Sly Stone: "We stopped by the Speakeasy, Revolution, even Jimi's Brook Street flat. After roaming all over London we finally gave up at about 3.00 am. The thought that kept drifting through my head afterwards was if only we could have found him, maybe he'd still be here."

Eric Clapton, who had long since become a soulmate of Jimi's took the news badly. "I was heartbroken and very angry. Nobody could be blamed, but I felt incredible fury. I loved Jimi and his music. We had a very close, intimate relationship. After his death I shut off my emotions towards Jimi because it was such devastation for me."

On 1st October, friends and family, including musicians Johnny Winter

ROW   SEAT

S 41

FLOOR

Retain Stub — Good Only

SAT.
8.00 P.M.   **MAY 3**

Davis Printing Limited

JIMI HENDRIX
EXPERIENCE
PRICE - - $5.50

ADMIT ONE. Entrance by Main
Door or by Church Street Door.

Maple Leaf Gardens
LIMITED

CONDITION OF SALE: Upon refund-
ing the purchase price the management may remove from the
person who has

Stora scenen, Liseberg

Tisdagen den 1 september 1970 kl. 20

Vi rekommenderar den ärade publiken att
infinna sig i god tid före programmets början.

Jimi Hendrix Experience

STÅPLATS

Kr. 15: —

(+ vanlig entre till parken)
Köpt biljett återlöses endast i händelse
av ändrad eller inställd föreställning.

№: 5040

HANDELSTRYCKERIET. GBG 701702

GRANADA
TOOTING

Sunday, APRIL 30th   8.30
DOORS OPEN AT 8.00 P.M.

Walker **2** Bros.
SHOW

CIRCLE 12/6

TICKETS CANNOT BE EXCHANGED OR MONEY
REFUNDED

ROW   B   35

Willsons (Printers) Ltd., Nottm.

SOPHIA GARDENS PAVILION
CARDIFF
Tel. CARDIFF 27657/8

HAROLD DAVISON and TITO BURNS
present

JIMI HENDRIX
and THE MOVE

THURSDAY, NOV. 23rd, 1967
2nd HOUSE 8-35 p.m.

PRICE 12/6

BLOCK   Row   Seat

B   E   31

No responsibility can
be accepted for lost   TO BE RETAINED
or unused tickets

13. I. 69   DM 14,00
incl.
Mehrwertsteuer

STADT KÖLN

Montag,
Einl

Lippn
THE
EXPERIEN
EIRE APPARENT

Veranstalter:
Örtl. Arrangement: Westdeutsche Konzertdirektion Köln

Kölner
Sport-
Halle

Keine Haftung für Sach- und Körperschäden.
Gelöste Karten werden nicht zurückgenommen. Beim Verlassen
der Halle verliert die Karte ihre Gültigkeit. Programm-Änderung
vorbehalten. Bei Vorverkauf 5% Aufschlag.

Innenraum   **SITZ NR.**
Block B   Reihe **6**   **03**

KAUFhOF bietet
tausendfach
alles unter
einem Dach

A 106
ORCHESTRA
CNTR

ATWOOD HALL
CLARK UNIVERSITY—WORCESTER, MASS.

MARCH
15
1968

Fri. Eve. at 8:15
Social Affairs Board
of Clark University
— PRESENTS —
THE
JIMI HENDRIX EXPERIENCE
ADMISSION $4.00

GOOD ONLY
FRIDAY EVE.
MARCH
15
1968

SLADE TICKET COMPANY

CNTR
A 106
ORCHESTRA
ATWOOD HALL

and Miles Davis, gathered at Seattle's Dunlap Baptist Church for a dignified and sombre service. Noel grimly recounts, "They had his body laid out in a coffin and we had to walk past it. I couldn't look. Mitch and I were both crying and held hands. They should have buried his white Fender guitar with him. It was his favorite."

After Jimi was laid to rest at Greenwood Cemetery in nearby Renton, his musical peers decided to grant him a wish he had often spoken of. "I tell you, when I die I'm not going to have a funeral, I'm going to have a jam session. I want people to just play my music, go wild and freak out."

Gerry Stickells, Jimi's longtime road manager and personal assistant,

Previous page, left: Jimi's last show in Sweden at the Stora Scenen-Liseberg, Gothenburg, 1st September, 1970.

Previous page, right: A collection of vintage concert tickets.

Opposite and above: Jimi at the Deutchlandhalle, Berlin, Germany, 4th September, 1970.

Above: Photo call on the Isle of Fehmarn, Germany, with Billy, Jimi and Mitch, 6th September, 1970 - only twelve days before Jimi's death.

Opposite: Jimi's final concert appearance on the Isle of Fehmarn, 6th September, 1970.

remembers, "We rented a hall and got a few instruments and the musicians got up and jammed. We had a good party. It was the way he would have wanted it. We gave him a good send-off."

In the wake of his death the inevitable tawdry exploitation began: the ugly, protracted battle over the Hendrix estate, the avalanche of bad bootlegs that flooded the market, the tabloid feast of grisly speculation over Jimi's demise, blaming everything from a heroin overdose to assassination plots and even hints of suicide. Much was made of Jimi's last poem written the night he died. Titled *The Story Of Life*, the final lines read:

> *"The story of life is quicker than the wink of an eye.*
> *The story of love is hello and goodbye*
> *Until we meet again."*

"Jimi's suicide note," Eric Burdon called it. Leon Hendrix gruffly countered, "That's no death poem. It's a life poem!"

Above: The funeral of James Marshall Hendrix, 1st October, 1970. Johnny Winter is on the far left, Chuck Wein is third from the left, and Mitch Mitchell with Noel Redding are at the extreme right.

Right: Miles Davis arrives at Jimi's funeral.

PROCLAMATION

WHEREAS, music plays a major role in all our lives -- a medium which moves us whether we are young, old, rich or poor, music is a part of us no matter our race, color, nation of origin, ability or sexual orientation; and

WHEREAS, Jimi Hendrix, pioneering guitarist, of the 1960's was born and raised in Seattle, Washington; and

WHEREAS, we are proud of the contributions of Seattle musicians who have risen to the top of their fields and delighted millions of listeners; and

WHEREAS, Jimi Hendrix died an untimely death and continues to be mourned by music lovers everywhere;

NOW, THEREFORE, I, NORMAN B. RICE, Mayor of the City of Seattle, do hereby proclaim, November 27, 1992 to be

JIMI HENDRIX DAY

in Seattle and encourage all citizens to remember the contributions he made to modern music.

Norman B. Rice
Mayor

Jimi Hendrix private rites set tomorrow

Private funeral services will be held tomorrow for Jimi Hendrix, the rock singing star who died in London September 28, a spokesman for the family said today.

The spokesman, Michael Goldstein, who was Hendrix' publicist, said the funeral is private and the family requests that the public stay away until after 4 p. m. Hendrix will be buried in Greenwood Cemetery, Renton, where, Goldstein said, the grave would be marked clearly for anyone who wishes to pay their respects.

The funeral will be at the Dunlap Baptist Church with the Rev. Harold A. Blackburn performing the ceremony. Mrs. Freddy Maye Gautier, a friend of the family, will read an obituary on behalf of the family.

Pall bearers will be David Anderson, James Thomas, Steve Phillips, Herbert Price, Eddy Howard and Danny Howell, all boyhood friends of Hendrix.

Goldstein said it was impossible to put together a memorial concert, planned for Sicks' Stadium, but added that many musicians and friends had offered to come.

He said the concert might be put together at a later date.

Over two decades later the fascination continues. Had he lived, where would Hendrix be today? Rock dinosaur or leader of musical change? All the evidence clearly points to the latter, for in one brief lifetime this brilliant, young artist virtually reinvented the blues, founded psychedelic funk and wandered boldly onto the cutting edge of an unprecedented jazz/classical/rock fusion. Perhaps in the end, like Janis Joplin, Jim Morrison and Brian Jones, Jimi Hendrix was just a shining traveller on a brief, glowing stop in the extraordinary sixties. "He'd gone through like a fireball without knowing it," Dylan once said.

Hendrix himself perhaps pointed to his own humble epitaph when he said: "Me, the world's greatest guitar player? That's silly. I'm just a messenger from God. Forget my name. My name is nothing but a distraction. Remember it only as a handshake."

Twenty-four years later, the world is still fondly remembering Jimi Hendrix and his music.

"He accomplished what he set out to do. I don't think he would have had it any other way." Al Hendrix

Above: Details of Jimi's funeral from a Seattle newspaper, 30th September, 1970.

Top: It's official! The Mayor of Seattle has proclaimed the 27th November JIMI HENDRIX DAY.

Appendix I: A Conversation between the author, Geoffrey Giuliano, and Jimi's father, James Allen Hendrix

Seattle, Washington, USA, 1982

A private snapshot with Al Hendrix from one of Jimi's infrequent visits home. Seattle, 6th September, 1968.

GG: Can you tell me something about your early life?

JAH: Well, I did want to get into the entertainment business. I'd been dancing ever since I can remember. Back then, people just put on shows, every once in a while. They knew me so they'd call and I'd get five or ten dollars for the night.

GG: So your mom and dad were in a minstrel show?

JAH: My mother was in showbusiness and my dad was too. He wasn't an entertainer, but my mother danced. There was me and my older brother, I was the youngest. My sister did a little dancing too, it was kind of all in the family.

GG: Did your parents make their living from showbusiness?

JAH: Oh yeah. In Seattle, around 1910, the show broke up and they went up to Canada to live. They lived in Seattle for a short while and then went to Vancouver.

GG: What about playing the spoons?

JAH: I just kind of picked it up from a fellow a long time ago. It's about the same thing as playing the bones. My dad had two pair of the red hardwood bones. Or you'd use spare rib bones, after you done cleaned 'em off.

GG: After dinner! Tell me about meeting Lucille.

JAH: It was kind of an accident. A girlfriend of

my room-mate brought her home and introduced me to her. I wasn't very excited because she was kind of young. I was doing some dancing that night so I asked if she wanted to come along. Anyway, I started going with her.

GG: What were you doing at the time?

JAH: I was working in a pool hall, I was the house man racking up the balls.

GG: The day you left for the army you got married to Lucille, is that right?

JAH: No, I got married about two or three days before, but it wasn't much.

GG: Wasn't her family against it?

JAH: Well her dad kind of made a noise about it,

but that wasn't no big thing. They sent me to Forest Hills, Oklahoma. I got my basic training there and then it was off to Fort Benning, Georgia. I was there for awhile and from there to Kamperka, Alabama.

GG: Was Lucille pregnant with Jimi before you left?

JAH: Yeah.

GG: Jimi once wrote, "The night I was born the moon turned a fire red."

JAH: Of course that was more or less fiction! In time of war, they told us, a soldier is allowed to go home on emergency furlough, death or births, but I was the furthest away from home in my outfit. So the commanding officer said, "Well you won't be able to go, because transportation is too slow." After chow they named all the guys that were going to the stockade and I was one of them. Anyway, I was in the stockade when Jimi was born. The next day I was put on the train for the west coast, out to Frisco.

GG: I understood there was some problem during the period you were gone between you and your wife, right? I don't want to get too personal, but you drifted apart and she left Jimi with some other people.

JAH: Yeah, he went to several different homes. Grandmother couldn't very well take care of him and my sister was having a hard time too. One woman, she died and her sister came up from Texas and took Jimi back to California. She had him after I got out of the service. I went down there and got him. One time when he was playing, Jimi asked me, "What was that woman's name?" I remembered it then, but I can't think of it now.

GG: After you were discharged you went to get Jimi? But the woman didn't want to turn Jimi loose, right?

JAH: She wrote me a letter and said, "We have fallen in love with Jimi and he's a part of the family. I want you to have this letter so you can show there won't be no controversy, no kind of way, shape or form. I know you want your son...." They had a picture of me I'd sent him and he used to say, "There's daddy."

GG: After you got Jimi where did you go?

JAH: I came right back to Seattle. I worked different types of jobs. After I came out of the service Lucille came back home. I said, "Well, I'll give it a go."

GG: So you were all together when Leon came along.

JAH: Yeah, but it started to break down. We got a divorce right away. Leon doesn't remember his mother because he was only about a year old. I got the kids. I had to settle down after all the running around I did in the service, like she did.

GG: Tell me about your son's name. It wasn't Jimi originally, was it?

JAH: His name was James Marshall. At one time it was Jimmy James, Maurice James and he had some other different handles in there too.

GG: When he was born, Lucille gave him the name of Johnny...

JAH: After I came home, I wanted to change that. I didn't like it.

GG: Tell me about the first time you ever had an idea that Jimi had some musical ability.

JAH: Jimi wasn't much of a dancer, or a singer. The first time he started singing he was playing somewhere back East and he told me, "Dad, I'm going to try some singing, everybody else is doing it. You know I can't hardly carry a tune." But then, there was a holler in him.

GG: In rock'n'roll a good voice sometimes works against you.

JAH: I've heard people mention, "Oh, I like to hear Jimi sing." Jimi was right though, he couldn't hold no tune. Personally, I used to mess around with the saxophone. That was about the time I bought his first guitar. Jimi probably knew more about the guitar than I knew about the sax, I just knew the scales. We were living in this old hotel and we'd sit up there, him plonking away and me blowing on the sax, trying to pick out the notes.

GG: How old was Jimi when he asked for a guitar?

JAH: One place where we were boarding this fellow had an old guitar and Jimi would be sitting out on the veranda plonking away. He offered to sell it to Jimi for five dollars or something. He wanted to try it out so I said, "Okay." He started learning a few things and got pretty good. Then I got him the electric guitar. He was staying out of trouble, off the streets.

GG: Who did he really get off on?

JAH: B.B. King, Muddy Waters, Chuck Berry...

GG: Everyone says Jimi Hendrix played white man's music, but actually he didn't.

JAH: He came out with a kind of psychedelic jazz, which was little heavy for the blacks. A lot of them didn't understand what was happening. It sounded a little strange. The first time I heard his record, we were living at the other place.

GG: What about practising, could he practise, did he get right into it?

JAH: Yeah, he used to practise every day when he came home from school. The first thing he'd do was pick up the guitar. I'd come home from work and he'd be playing to a lot of records. He'd be playing along with them or getting ideas. Watching TV, he'd plonk away during the commercials. His friends would come by or he'd go to their place.

GG: What did they call him then?

JAH: Well, he had a nickname when he was small. It was 'Buster' and that stuck for a long time until he was around ten. He turned to me one day and said, "Dad, I want you to start calling me Jimi." He started telling his friends to call him Jimi, too.

GG: Did he ever take any guitar lessons?

JAH: Maybe some friends may have shown him a few things, but there was never any regular music teacher.

GG: How old was he when he first got into a group?

JAH: I guess he was around fifteen or sixteen. They had different little groups, he used to play for picnics and at parties.

GG: How much would they make?

JAH: Well sometimes it would be almost ten dollars for the engagement, ten dollars a piece, though it was seldom worked out that way. Jimi used to get so mad, he'd come home with three dollars or something. I remember one time they had to pay five dollars for the jackets they wore. I got a picture of him in it just before he took it back to the rental place. He didn't make any money on that gig. He'd say, "Oh, I ain't gonna play with those guys no more." They'd get together and do an engagement, it wasn't a big thing. It was just a bunch of kids he'd get together. He had three or four different groups. Sometimes they'd have two guitars, it wasn't like the groups are now, just a bunch of guys getting together to play.

GG: One thing that Jimi Hendrix was famous for, he loved good looking women.

JAH: Actually, he was kind of shy with girls then.

GG: I heard a story that he got beat up when some guy thought Jimi was going out with his girlfriend. They went in the bathroom and Jimi didn't fight back. When he came out he was all bloody and went on and did the show.

JAH: Sometimes he had little fights, but the girls were always coming around the house.

GG: Can you tell me the story about when he told you what was going to happen in the future.

JAH: We were in the house on a Friday with his brother. I got done from work and he said, "Some day you're gonna take it easy, because I'm going to be famous." I said, "Hurry up." I was laughing. I figured that he was going to make it, but internationally, I didn't. When he first came home he kept saying, "Oh yeah, it's been five years since I've been here." He'd been home I think three times when he was in the service. When I first heard from him he told me that he had a medical discharge and he didn't want to come home. He wanted to make a name for himself because he'd been playing around with different groups.

GG: Let's go back to when Jimi started getting into a little bit of trouble during high school and he quit.

JAH: Well, he was just more or less a visitor at school. He used to miss a lot of days.

GG: That must have worried you, didn't it?

JAH: Not a whole lot as long as he wasn't in trouble.

GG: Was he a respectful boy?

JAH: He didn't back talk to me.

GG: How do you get along with Leon?

JAH: We get along okay. They got separated

Jimi and his dad jam together just like they used to do when Jimi was growing up. Seattle, 23rd May, 1969.

after I was out of work. It was only Jimi and I together. Leon had to go one of these foster places and come home weekends. He wasn't with us all the time so they grew up separate in that way. Jimi and I though were together all the time.

GG: Tell me about Jimi going into the service.

JAH: Well, he was going to be drafted anyway. He went to the recruiting office and the Sergeant explained to him if he were to volunteer now, he'd get whatever choice of service he wanted. That's why he went in. Jimi wanted to get one of these Screaming Eagle badges, so he volunteered.

GG: They say that his buddies in the army would say, "Man, that guy is weird, he sleeps with his guitar!"

JAH: He wasn't allowed to have the guitar in basic training which was eight weeks. After that he wrote me and said, "Well, dad, can you send me my guitar?"

GG: The first time he jumped out of an airplane, was that a big day for him?

JAH: He didn't call many times. He didn't have the money to call so he used to do a lot of writing. He sent me some pictures of him jumping and he'd be taking pictures of the other guys.

GG: Did he have a band in the army?

JAH: He met Billy Cox and I know he met other musicians when he'd get weekend passes and went to town.

GG: When he left the service where did he go?

JAH: He was bouncing around to a whole lot of different places, playing Nashville. He was scuffling around more or less. It was good when Charles Chandler asked him to go to London.

GG: The thing about Jimi's that many people always felt he had some kind of magic power.

JAH: When he died one guy called up and said, "Why didn't you go down to the funeral home and check his body. He might have been in suspended animation because he had this magic." I said, "Wait a minute, Jimi was just a plain ordinary person."

GG: He once sang, "If I don't meet you no more in this world, I'll see you in the next one."

JAH: People ask, "What was Jimi like when he was a kid, playing his guitar and you sitting there listening to him." They almost felt like...

GG: He was Jesus or something...

JAH: Yeah, he had a halo around his head. If Jimi was doing something bad he'd get a whipping just like anybody else.

GG: If you counted everything up, you've been robbed for millions, right?

JAH: I know a lot of the things Jimi had and all

that was ripped off. Just like his belt. That cost five hundred dollars. I remember him telling me about that belt the first time he came home. He said, "Daddy, do you know how much this belt cost?" I said, "I have no idea," but I could see all this turquoise in there and he said, "I had it made by the Navajo Indians." I haven't seen his belt since his death.

GG: What about all of his papers, his poems, his drawings, all of that was in London and disappeared.

JAH: There was a whole lot of jewelry he had, an elephant necklace, he showed it to me when we were going up to Vancouver, he had it around his neck, all the different rings. They were all lost.

GG: Can you tell me how you heard about Jimi's death?

JAH: We were still in bed when Jimi's attorney called from New York and told us about it. Then not long after I got up and it came on the radio.

GG: Finally, what do you think about all the bootlegs and questionable compilations that have come out in the past few years.

JAH: It's like an unfinished painting by Michelangelo. Somebody else comes along and finishes it off. That's the same with Jimi's records. They couldn't think the way Jimi did on how to finish it. What they had in mind Jimi wouldn't go for.

Appendix II: Selected Jimi Hendrix Discography

Due to space limitations only the most historically significant releases are listed here.

An assortment of CD insets from around the world.

Official releases

Are You Experienced? (1967)
Axis: Bold As Love (1967)
Smash Hits (1968 and 1969)
Electric Ladyland (1968)
Band Of Gypsys (1970)
The Cry Of Love (1971)
Rainbow Bridge (1971)
Isle Of Wight (1971)
Experience (1971)
More Experience (1971)
Hendrix In The West (1972)
War Heroes (1972)
Sound Track Recordings From The Film Jimi Hendrix (1973)
Loose Ends (1974)
Crash Landing (1975)
Midnight Lightning (1975)
The Essential Jimi Hendrix (1978)
The Essential Jimi Hendrix Volume Two (1979)
Nine To The Universe (1980)
The Jimi Hendrix Concerts (1982 and 1989)
The Singles Album (1983)
Kiss The Sky (1984)
Jimi Plays Monterey (1986)
Band Of Gypsys 2 (1986)
Johnny B. Goode (1986)
Live At Winterland (1987)
Radio One (1988)
Live & Unreleased (1989)
Variations On A Theme: Red House (1989)
Cornerstone 1967-1970 (1990)
Hendrix Speaks (1990)
Lifelines (1990)
Sessions (1990)
Footlights (1991)
Stages (1991)
Calling Long Distance... (1992)
The Ultimate Experience (1992)
Blues (1994)
Woodstock (1994)

Jimi Hendrix As Guest Artist and/or Producer

Get That Feeling (with Curtis Knight, 1967)

Flashing (with Curtis Knight, 1968)
The Great Jimi Hendrix In New York (with Curtis Knight, 1968)
McGough & McGear (1968)
Sunrise (with Eire Apparent, 1969)
Cat Mother And The All Night Newsboys (1969)
You Can Be Anyone This Time Around (with Timothy Leary, 1970)
Stephen Stills (1970)
False Start (with Love, 1970)
Two Great Experiences Together (with Lonnie Youngblood, 1971)
In The Beginning (with The Isley Brothers, 1971)
Early Jimi Hendrix (with Curtis Knight, 1971)
Early Jimi Hendrix Vol II (with Curtis Knight, 1971)
In The Beginning (with Curtis Knight, 1973)
Doriella Du Fontaine (with Lightnin' Rod, 1984)

continued overleaf

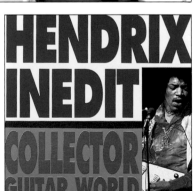

Bootlegs

Live At The Los Angeles Forum 4-25-70 (1970)
Live Experience 1967-68 (1970)
This Flyer (1970)
Good Vibes (early 1970's)
Live At Philharmonic Hall (early 1970's)
Live In Stockholm (early 1970's)
Incident At Rainbow Bridge (1971)
Good Karma 1 (1972)
Good Karma 2 (1973)
Can You Here [sic] Me Rock (mid 1970's)
Guitar Hero (1977)
Last British Concert (1980)
Electric Church Music Part 1 (1981)
The Good Die Young (1981)
Live In Ottaway [sic] (1981)
Davenport, Iowa '68 (1982)
The Lord Of The Strings (1983)
Live At The Hollywood Bowl (mid 1980's)
Sir James Marshall Gypsy On Cloud Nine (mid 1980's)
You Can't Use My Name (mid 1980's)
Wink Of An Eye (mid 1980's)
Electric Birthday Jimi (1987)
First Rays Of The Rising Sun (1987)
This One's For You (1987)
Paris 67 (1987)
A Lifetime Of Experience (1988)
Café Au Go Go (1988)
Fuckin' His Guitar For Denmark (1988)
Gypsy Suns, Moons And Rainbows (1988)
Loaded Guitar (1988)
Star Spangled Blues (1988)
The Wild Man Of Pop Plays Volume 1 (1988)
The Wild Man Of Pop Plays Volume 2 (1988)
Acoustic Jams (1989)
Atlanta (1989)
L.A. Forum (1989)
The Legendary Starclub Tapes (1989)
The Master's Masters (1989)
Midnight Magic (1989)
On The Killing Floor (1989)
The Things I Used To Do (1989)
The Winterland Days (1989)
Electric Hendrix 1 (1990)
Electric Hendrix 2 (1990)
It Never Takes An End... (1990)

Jimi Hendrix & Traffic A Session (1990)
Cherokee Mist (1991)
Riots In Berkeley (1991)
Band Of Gypsies Vol. 3 (1992)
Happy New Year, Jimi (1992)
Flaming Guitar (1993)
The First Rays Of The New Rising Sun (1993)
Lost Winterland Tapes (1993)
Multicoloured Blues: The Unreleased Sessions (1993)
1968 A.D. (1993)
Out Of The Studio: Demo's From 1967 (1993)
Spicy Essence: Apartment Jam 70 (1993)
Studio Haze (1993)
Axis Bold As Love: The Sotheby's Reels (1994)
The Berkeley Concerts II: The Sound Checks (1994)
Freak Out Blues (1994)
Free Concert (1994)
Shokan Sunrise (1994)

A collection of bootleg covers.

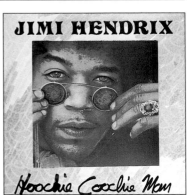

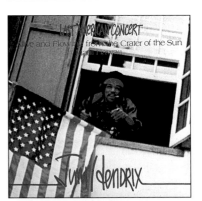

Appendix III: A Conversation between the author, Geoffrey Giuliano, and Noel Redding

Republic of Ireland, January 1994

Jimi and Noel Redding at the Hotel Opalen, Gothenburg, 3rd January, 1968.

GG: In your book *Are You Experienced?*, you say you were told that a French hit man killed Jimi. Is that correct?

NR: Someone told me that. I can't remember where it was - I'd have to think about it. Some guy said, 'Oh yeah, there was this German hit man sent in and he killed Jimi." I said, 'Oh really?' I was wondering how it was done.

GG: And did he tell you?

NR: No. And there again, you have to consider these things, because our French royalties never reached the band anyway. They were sent to a company in Aruba in the Dutch Antilles.

GG: Do you think it is possible, knowing what you know, that Jimi Hendrix was murdered?

NR: I would say it is possible. Someone could have slipped him a Mickey Finn, but I could be wrong. I've got the coroner's report and he said

that there was an unidentified substance in his body. So what was that? Because I've been tracing what he took.

GG: And so the conclusion you've come to after all these years is that you think it's possible and/or probable that Jimi was murdered?

NR: I'd say possible, but I could be completely wrong.

GG: If he was murdered, then the next logical question is why?

NR: Because, at that point, his career wasn't going too well and he'd be better off dead. The last tour of Europe was awful.

GG: During a previous conversation which we had, you said that you felt in many ways Jimi could have been more valuable dead than alive.

NR: Yeah. There was a big blowout because Electric Lady Studios was bought out of our royal-

ties. I gather, via Michael Jeffery, that they got a loan to set up the studio in lieu of the royalties. But they were going down a bit because he hadn't done much.

GG: I've heard there are over six hundred hours of unreleased Hendrix material about. Is it possible that people might have thought, 'If we bump the guy off, then we don't have to deal with him. It'll be much easier to deal with a dead artist than a live one and then we can do whatever we want with the tapes.' Does that seem reasonable?

NR: I suppose so, yeah.

GG: How do you feel about all of the posthumous releases?

NR: I think they're awful, because the band only made about three albums anyway.

GG: Was there an insurance policy on Jimi's life?

NR: That's right. Jeffery got a million dollars ....

Jimi and Noel arrive at Seattle Airport, 23rd May, 1969.

I've heard that when Jeffery died, the money went to his father, who I gather is still alive. It's sitting in a bank in London somewhere, held because of all the question marks.

GG: How do you feel about the investigation into Jimi's death being re-opened?

NR: I welcome it personally. I can rest easier and I think it would be great for everyone to rest easy.

GG: In a nutshell how was Jeffery ripping off Hendrix?

NR: All the monies were being sent to an off-shore company called Yamenta in the Bahamas.

GG: What was Jeffery's relationship with Hendrix? Did he hate him? Did Jimi want to get away from him?

NR: Well, I'd been out of the band for a while, but I think it all stemmed from the Electric Lady deal. I have all this on paper. Hendrix had to reproduce what he was producing before. And the last year of his life, as you said, he had six hundred hours of tape and they were using our royalties as collateral for the big loans.

GG: I've read that Jeffery never forgave Jimi because he slept with his girlfriend.

NR: That could have been possible.

GG: What was your opinion of Mike Jeffery as a manager?

NR: Well, he was always alright with me. I remember when I left the band and I did the Fat Mattress thing, I signed with Chas Chandler and

Jeffery said to me, 'I could sue you.' But he didn't. He was always very polite to me.

GG: Do you think he was a crook?

NR: He was obviously a crook, what about all his clubs in Spain?

GG: What about them?

NR: Well, there were all these clubs which were bought with money from The Experience. What happened to all that money?

GG: Did Jimi ever complain to you about the deal you were getting from Jeffery?

NR: I was normally the person who complained about the financial situation. I'd be the guy who'd write a letter to like, Chas, this is early on. I've investigated a lot of people and come up against brick walls. I've got loads of files.

GG: Tom Keylock from The Rolling Stones management was telling me that Jimi used to have to borrow money for cabs and dinner from Brian Jones as he was that skint.

NR: Yeah, that would be right, when we were in London and didn't have much money. I know that Jimi actually went to Harold Davidson from the agency and had to borrow five hundred pounds, and Mitch and I went to Track Records and we were given six hundred pounds between us.

GG: I have some old bank statements of Jimi's, which prove that, at the very height of his success, he had only two or three hundred pounds in the bank. How can three internationally heralded

rock stars be so skint?

NR: Because we were told, 'Don't worry lads, it's all being taken care of. The money's gone to the Bahamas so you won't have to pay tax on it, and you can collect it later.'

GG: How did you feel when you heard that Jeffery was dead?

NR: It was very strange, because that night I had a dream that Jimi came down and I was talking to him. I said, 'You're dead,' and he said 'Well, I've just come to see someone.' The next day I had a call from my sister in England saying that Jeffery had been killed.

GG: Have you ever heard about this alleged kidnapping of Jimi?

NR: I heard about it after the fact. I think it was probably a couple of years later.

GG: What do you think about the possibility that Jeffery knew he was going to lose Hendrix, so he kidnapped him in order to save him and then say, 'Hey look, I saved you, you should be grateful and stay with me.'?

NR: Perhaps.

GG: Would you put it past Jeffery?

NR: No.

GG: You obviously don't have a very high opinion of him.

NR: Well, he never threatened me. Personally, he was always very polite.

Poster for the biopic released by Warner Bros, in 1973.

THE MAGIC OF **J**IMI **H**ENDRIX, perhaps the greatest musical visionary of this century, continues to touch many hearts.

Today, twenty-four years after his death, Hendrix maintains a loyal following as evidenced by the highly esteemed publication *UniVibes - International Jimi Hendrix Magazine*, handsomely produced by Hendrix authority, Caesar Glebbeek (founder of the Hendrix Information Centre in 1967 and co-author of the 1990 definitive biography *Jimi Hendrix: Electric Gypsy*, published in the UK, USA, Italy and Germany).

Interested persons may write to: UniVibes, Coppeen, Enniskeane, County Cork, Republic of Ireland

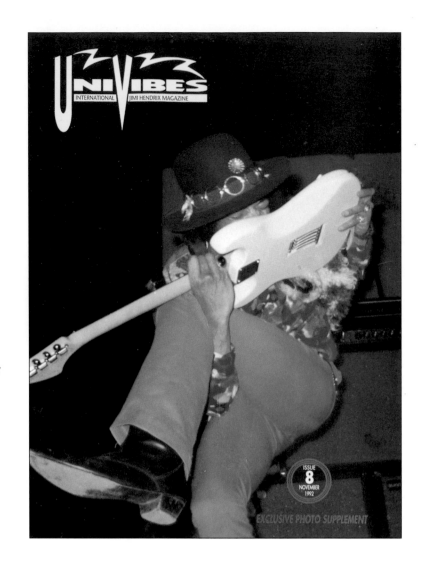

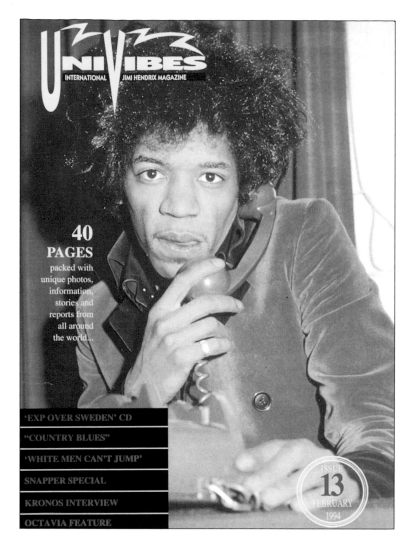

UNIVIBES
INTERNATIONAL JIMI HENDRIX MAGAZINE

40 PAGES
packed with unique photos, information, stories and reports from all around the world...

'EXP OVER SWEDEN' CD

"COUNTRY BLUES"

'WHITE MEN CAN'T JUMP'

SNAPPER SPECIAL

KRONOS INTERVIEW

OCTAVIA FEATURE

ISSUE **13** FEBRUARY 1994

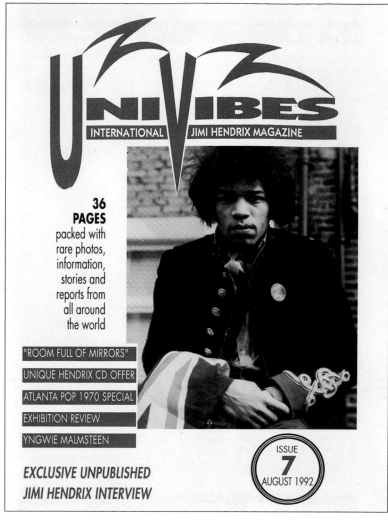

UNIVIBES
INTERNATIONAL JIMI HENDRIX MAGAZINE

36 PAGES
packed with rare photos, information, stories and reports from all around the world

"ROOM FULL OF MIRRORS"

UNIQUE HENDRIX CD OFFER

ATLANTA POP 1970 SPECIAL

EXHIBITION REVIEW

YNGWIE MALMSTEEN

EXCLUSIVE UNPUBLISHED JIMI HENDRIX INTERVIEW

ISSUE **7** AUGUST 1992

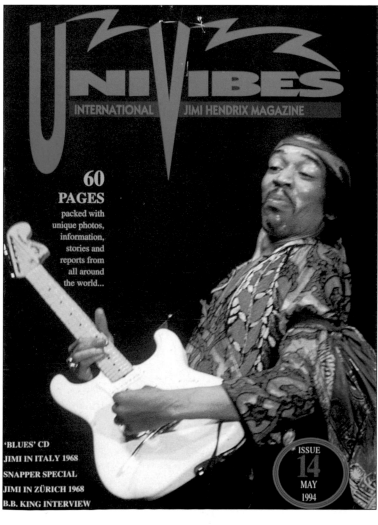

UNIVIBES
INTERNATIONAL JIMI HENDRIX MAGAZINE

60 PAGES
packed with unique photos, information, stories and reports from all around the world...

'BLUES' CD
JIMI IN ITALY 1968
SNAPPER SPECIAL
JIMI IN ZÜRICH 1968
B.B. KING INTERVIEW

ISSUE **14** MAY 1994

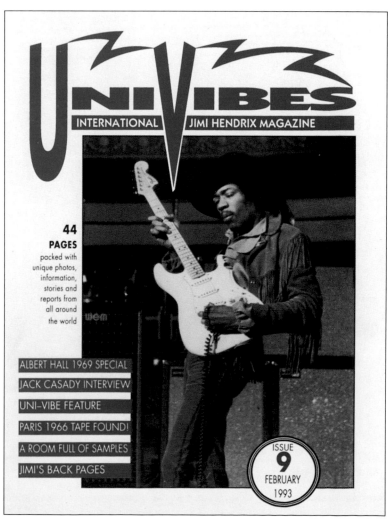

UNIVIBES
INTERNATIONAL JIMI HENDRIX MAGAZINE

44 PAGES
packed with unique photos, information, stories and reports from all around the world

ALBERT HALL 1969 SPECIAL

JACK CASADY INTERVIEW

UNI-VIBE FEATURE

PARIS 1966 TAPE FOUND!

A ROOM FULL OF SAMPLES

JIMI'S BACK PAGES

ISSUE **9** FEBRUARY 1993

Acknowledgements

Senior Editors: Brenda Giuliano and Sara Colledge
Executive Researcher: Sesa Nichole Giuliano
Intern: Devin Giuliano
Photo Research: Caesar Glebbeek/*UniVibes*

The authors would like to thank the following people for their kindness in helping to publish this book.

Sriman Jagannatha Dasa Adikari
Dr. Mirza Beg
Deni Bouchard
Stefano Castino
Srimati Vrinda Rani Devi Dasi
Enzo of Valentino
Robin Scot Giuliano
Avalon and India Giuliano
ISKCON
Tim Hailstone

Suneel Jaitly
Jo Messham
Marcus Lecky
His Divine Grace B.H. Mangalniloy Goswami
Dr. Michael Klapper
Leaf Leavesley
Donald Lehr
Timothy Leary
Andrew Lownie
Mark Studios, Clarence, New York
His Divine Grace A.C. Bhaktivedanta Swami
Prabhupada
Steven Rosen
Self Realization Institute of America (SRI)

Wendell and Joan Smith
Something Fishy Productions Ltd.
Dave Thompson
Edward Veltman
Robert Wallace
Dr. Ronald Zucker

Photo credits

Caesar Glebbeek: 38, 39 (top, bottom), 54 (below), 57, 58.
Caesar Glebbeek collection: 21, 29, 31, 32, 33 (right), 34, 36 (left), 37 (right), 39(below right), 48 (left), 49 (below), 50 (right), 55, 60, 62 (below), 70, 71 (below), 73, 75, 76, 79 (also contributed by Robert Echter collection/second from bottom. Bob Elliot collection/top left - & Dennis Johansson collection/top right), 82, 83, 89, 90.
Al Hendrix collection: half title page, 8, 9, 10, 11, 12, 13, 14, 15, 17, 18, 19, 48 (right), 52 (top), 53 (left), 59 (below left), 84, 86, 88.
Axis Archives collection: 6, 8, 16 (left), 40, 47, 52 (below), 61, 67, 93, 96.
Bildservice: 35, 43, 44, 46, 54 (top), 77, 78, 91.
Ben Valkhoff collection: 26, 27, 59 (top right).
Square Circle Archives: 36 (right), 37 (left), 49 (top).
BMS Platt: cover
Jess Hansen collection: 85 (left).
Pearl Brown collection: 7, 16 (right).
Ulrich Handl: 24.
DPA: 30.
Polydor: 56, 80.
John Goddard: 33 (left).
Peter Herzig collection: 50 (left).
RDZ: 51 (left).
Snaps Unlimited: 51 (right).
UPI: 59 (top left), 65.
Doug Carr: 59 (below right).
Grant H. Reid: 62 (top), 63.
Warner Bros: 64, 69.
Antahkarana Archives: 71 (top).
Ron Theisen collection: 72.
Central Press: 74
Key Archives: 81
Pandis: title page.

JIMI'S LAST LOST DAYS

NOW 20 SEP 70

"I NEED HELP BAD, MAN." These words, gasped into a telephone-answering machine in an empty office, are the epitaph of Jimi Hendrix, idol of millions and prophet-in-chief of the drug generation.

EXCLUSIVE by Simon Regan

They were spoken at 1.30 on Friday morning and discovered on the tape when the office opened at 10 a.m.

Charles Chandler of the Robert ... business ... drix's ... made a ... to the ... ber the ... given ...

But, ... addict ... death ... later, m ...

Within ... dead. A ... the pop ... he helped perpetuate.

I have pieced together the incredible last three days of Hendrix's life—the days in which he was missing from his £17-a-day suite in London's Cumberland Hotel.

Millions

Hendrix had come up in the pop world at a breathtaking pace.

'One minute he was just another coloured musician in the dives of Greenwich Village, New York's hippie Mecca. An ex-U.S. Marine, the son of a Cherokee Indian and a Negress.

HENDRIX
me late...

I saw Jimi dying

Continued from Page One

Organised Crimes Branch. It was triggered by a plea for a new inquest by another former girlfriend of Hendrix, Kathy Etchingham. She commissioned a private investigation into the case and sent a dossier on the findings to the Attorney General.

Miss Etchingham has always claimed: 'The death was all very dodgy. I don't think it should have happened. He was in the wrong place at the wrong time with the wrong people.'

Miss Danneman, who lives on the South Coast, has said that Hendrix fans still blame her for the death. She recently hired her own private detective to prove that she did all she could to save him.

She wept at the inquest in September 1970, as she told Westminster coroner Gavin Thurston how Hendrix came to stay with her four days before his death.

On their last day together, a Thursday, they took photographs and went shopping, she said. 'He went to his hotel to make a telephone call to New York,' said Miss Dannemann. 'He came home at 8.30pm. I cooked a meal and we drank a bottle of white wine. He drank rather more than I did, but he was not a drinking man.

'There was no arguing or stress. We were talking and listening to music.' The following morning she woke at 10.20am and wanted some cigarettes. 'But as Jimi did not like me going out without me telling him, I looked to see if he was awake. He was sleeping normally. Just before I was about to go out I looked at him again and realised he was ill. I tried to wake him up but I couldn't. Then I saw he had been taking some of my sleeping tablets.

'He must have taken them shortly after I started to go to sleep.'

She told the inquest that she had never known the guitarist to take hard drugs, although he had admitted trying them. 'He was never sad or depressed when he was with me,' she concluded.

Even in an era which revelled in excess, Hendrix contrived to be shocking.

The establishment on both sides of the Atlantic recoiled in horror as he shot to superstardom in a barrage of electronic feedback and sexual imagery.

The story began in Seattle in 1942. James Marshall Hendrix was born the son of a gardener, an exotic cocktail of Cherokee Indian, Mexican and black.

He left school early and hitched around the States with his guitar before arriving in New York, backing the Isley Brothers and touring as an anonymous musician with big names including Tina Turner.

He was spotted playing for £10 a night in Greenwich Village by Chas Chandler, a former member of the Animals, who

... to Notting Hill and smoked pot at various pads in West London. "Jimi was completely out of his mind.

"One man we met up with was so out of his mind with drugs that he jumped over the banisters of a house and was carted off to hospital with broken legs.

"When all this commotion happened Jimi went mad and ran around the house shouting."

All day Thursday, Hendrix lay unconscious in the flat of a girl friend in Redcliffe Gardens, Fulham.

... ambula... hospita...

And ... the 14-... most e... musicia... delight... making... on sta...

Yeste... reporte... drix's ... weird ... up in ...

Fans ... and he... ing an... discotheques played Hendrix records non-stop.

Monika Dannemann: She recently hired a private detective to prove that she did everything possible to save Hendrix

persuaded him to try his luck in England where he put together a three-piece group called the Jimi Hendrix Experience.

His 'freaked out' hair and wild stage act, which included playing guitar with his teeth, catapulted him to fame in 1967 with his first hit, Hey Joe.

The burning of his guitar onstage at the Monterey Festival and his screamingly distorted rendition of the Star Spangled Banner at Woodstock assured his status.

Two weeks before he died at the age of 27, he played at the Isle of Wight...

The day ... he was ... Scott's ...

One of ... nessed ... session ... formerly ... He said ... 'Monika ... an accident ... think it's ... to use d... think he ... destroyed ...

Last mo... man said ... pared to ... the police ... firm to ... has been ...